MY Cosmic HAMMER

by KRISTIN PIERCE

Inner Compass
Books

Cover Photo and Author Photo Credit: Nancy Newby
Edited by Tami Stark and Lacy Lieffers of One Leaf Editing
Interior Layout by Heidi Strelioff of Blue Bean Design
Cover Design by Kristin Pierce

ISBN:
Paperback: 9781999088156
eBook: 9781999088149

Inner Compass Books 2020

Inner C⊛mpass
Books.com

DEDICATION:

To Mom: You were right by my side for every blood test, doctor's appointment, needle prick, swipe of the hair clippers, exploding vein, bag of chemo, and blood transfusion. Thank you for being there and for doing whatever it took to help me endure the hardest time of my life. I appreciate you and all you did for me, even if I didn't voice it enough at the time.

To Dad: You would have done anything under the sun to ease my pain. Thank you for speaking up for me when I needed it, for drinking the "clean out" juice when I couldn't stomach it, and for sneaking me Easy Mac to cure my post-surgical hunger pangs. That's love right there.

To my brothers: Your presence, compassion, and laughter-inducing twin shenanigans were more helpful and healing than you'll know. Thank you for showing up and spending time with me while I was sick.
I am proud to be your big sister.

INTRODUCTION

In 2007, at the age of twenty-one, I was handed a diagnosis that changed every piece of me—cancer. As an elite athlete on a volleyball scholarship, I was completely blindsided. How could this happen to someone so young and physically healthy?

Well, there was a lot more going on underneath the physically fit human suit I was walking around in. There's always more than meets the eye. This is the story of my own cosmic hammer experience that shook me until I crumbled on the floor. Brutal, terrifying, and exhausting, the summer of 2007 opened up my incredibly logical mind to discover who I truly was underneath all of the rules, labels, roles, masks and expectations I was constantly forcing myself live up to and fit into.

Thirteen years later, I am still unpacking lessons from the most challenging experience of my life. Up until November 2019, I hadn't considered writing about my story. Instead, when asked about it, I neatly shared my abbreviated experience so as to not offend anyone, who might have had it worse, with my perspective. But, as we peel the layers back, we simultaneously peel open our minds, eyes, and hearts to new perspectives, which allows us to see new possibilities that have been patiently waiting for our wits to grow sharper.

Why now? You might be wondering. And trust me, I've had that question rattling around in my brain since I started writing this book. The short answer is that it was finally time to fully and wholly unpack the excruciating experience that served as the turning point for my entire life. Cancer was a huge wake-up call that was delivered with impeccable timing—I just didn't have the capacity to understand that at the time. As trying as it was, there were (and still are) incredible lessons to unwrap.

My Cosmic Hammer

I could start this book by placing blame on the people, places, and things that may or may not have contributed to having cancer—but, passing the blame is not how we heal, and my experience was by my own design. We are complex beings full of thoughts, emotions, beliefs, experiences, and memories that colour our own personal lens and mold us into the people we become. We are a culmination of so many experiences, which makes it impossible to narrow down the cause of disease to any one thing. And when we blame, we only give our power away.

Taking personal responsibility for our lives is the only way to create change. Every experience is happening for us— like stepping stones that lead us back home to ourselves. Each experience has within it learning, growth, and lessons to unwrap. I understand that it can be incredibly difficult to accept that statement. It took me a long time to fully understand why I needed the cosmic hammer of cancer and how it could have possibly happened to help me. But, the layers of learning continue to reveal themselves. And over time, my self-blame has turned into self-understanding and self-compassion, especially as I've wrestled with writing this memoir.

While I used to think I was blindsided by cancer, the more I have unpacked this cosmic hammer, the more I realized that we can only be blindsided when we aren't paying attention. Cancer didn't come out of thin air. It was a build-up of beliefs, suppressed emotions, and internal mental warfare. Physically, yes—I was blindsided by cancer, because at the time I was doing everything that was considered to be "right" to maintain my physical health. However, there is so much more to health than the physical body. So much more. And that was something I had to learn the hard way.

Ultimately, I've written this book because I'm ready to heal my story. I'm ready to accept my whole self: my experience, my journey, and my story. I'm ready to stop shaming myself for this experience like I was asking for it. It's time to stop downplaying this part of my life. My kids are starting to ask questions, and I don't want them to feel scared, which means that I can't be scared to share this part of my life. Because it happened. And even though it was devastating, it was also the start of an incredible unbecoming that has led me to unravel and discover who I really am. As Brene Brown says, "Loving ourselves through the process of owning our story is the bravest thing we will ever do."

CONTENTS

PART I: RUMBLING..1

    STRONG AS A MOTHER..2

    FEAR HAS A PURPOSE..5

    REBIRTH-DAY..8

    A FEAR EPIDEMIC...14

    FEAR FEEDS CANCER...17

    LUCKY THIRTEEN..20

    COSMIC HAMMERS...23

PART II: MY COSMIC HAMMER..27

    MISS INDEPENDENT...29

    MENTAL TOUGHNESS..32

    FULL RIDE...34

    THREE-A-DAYS..37

    BEER CART GIRL + PRO SHOP BOY........................39

    MY BODY WHISPERED..41

    CAMPUS DOCTOR...45

    RAISED ON WESTERN MEDICINE............................47

    SPRINGFEST...49

    LAND OF LIVING SKIES...52

    WHISPERS BECOME SCREAMS.................................55

    SPITFIRE PEP TALK...60

    THE PHONE CALL...62

    HOMETOWN HOSPITAL HOPE..................................66

    WHATEVER IT TAKES..69

    TWENTY WEEKS..71

    LET'S TALK ABOUT SEX...76

    A PLETHORA OF TESTS...77

    DEMEROL FIRE..79

    THIS DOESN'T MAKE SENSE.....................................82

    STENT SURGERY...84

    THE BODY TALKS...87

    IT TAKES A VILLAGE...94

    LIGHTEN UP 97

    GASTRO CLEAN OUT...99

    THE DOCTOR IS IN...103

THE POWER OF A DIAGNOSIS...108

THE BIG DAY 111

WHOSE BODY IS THIS?..115

DON'T BE A HERO...119

CREAM OF (NO) POTATO...121

SHE'S SO FLUFFY...123

THE SPACE BETWEEN...125

NERF GUN..129

NOTHING TO BLAME...133

DIESEL..135

THE CANCER CENTRE...138

CHEMO 101..142

ARM CANDY..146

BUZZ CUTS..151

ON THE FIRST DAY OF CHEMO.......................................153

INJECTION REFLECTIONS..160

FEVER EMERGENCY...163

MUSIC IS HEALING..169

IT ALL FALLS DOWN...172

WIGGIN' OUT...180

BALD DOESN'T FEEL BEAUTIFUL..................................184

CORN POPS & MONSTER COOKIES.................................189

FRIENDS FOR KEEPS...192

I WANT MY MOM..197

LOOK GOOD, FEEL BETTER...205

BLOODY HELL...207

A CASE OF THE EXPLODING VEINS................................210

HOMESTRETCH HALLELUJAH.......................................215

FIRST TASTE OF FREEDOM..218

PART III: CONNECTING THE DOTS.............................**221**

WESTERN MEDICINE SAVED MY LIFE............................222

THE MEANING OF CANCER..225

THE OTHER SIDE..228

MY WAKE-UP CALL..230

MOMENTS..233

ACKNOWLEDGEMENTS...235

ABOUT THE AUTHOR..239

PART ONE:

Rumbling

"Our job is not to deny the story, but to defy the ending—to rise strong, recognize our story, and rumble with the truth until we get to a place where we think, Yes. This is what happened. This is my truth. And I will choose how the story ends."
– Brené Brown

STRONG AS A MOTHER

"A mind that opens up to a new idea never returns to its original size."
– Albert Einstein

In November of 2019, I sat on a panel alongside three other Saskatchewan female authors at the Strong as a Mother event hosted by Laura of MindBody Balance Therapies in Melfort, Saskatchewan. As we discussed the power of our voices, I listened with admiration as the other authors spoke of how writing about their experiences was both healing and transformative. Since I quite enjoy the therapeutic benefits of journaling and writing to help me sort through my thoughts, their accounts didn't surprise me. But the light bulb moment came when I heard how the attendees had been moved, transformed, and impacted by reading these authors' personal stories.

*A memoir that transforms someone else...*Why did this idea seem so foreign to me?

I had just released my third children's picture book a couple weeks prior, with big plans for more. Up until that night, I had never considered writing anything other than empowering children's books that were designed to inspire young minds.

That night, the Strong as a Mother event cracked me open. It showed me that stories can connect us, transform us, and give us permission to change our minds and our lives. That is pretty damn powerful. My mind was stretched to a new possibility, and I was moved by the courage these women displayed in baring their souls. In witnessing the impact and transformations being discussed all around me, I wondered why I hadn't considered writing about my experience with cancer.

Quite simply, it had literally never dawned on me to do so. Of course, my experience was impactful—it had completely changed the course of my life, along with my perspective, my mindset, and my understanding of myself. But, why had I never considered writing a book about it?

Huh. I thought. *A memoir, hey?* This possibility had never dawned on me before. I was surprised but nodded my head and tried to stay present in the panel conversation.

When I was asked about my story, I "politely" got my point across while intensely abbreviating it so as to not infringe on the other authors' time. I recognized I had done this when the other panel members went on to share much more detailed experiences. What was that about? I wondered. Why do I always do that? Over the years of being asked how I got into BodyTalk or teaching MindScape or writing, I had weeded my entire "story" down to a mere few sentences. Was I being succinct? Or, was I scared to truly speak up?

I drifted into MindScape where a twenty-one-year-old version of myself sat with her knees pulled in toward her chest. Her long, blonde hair was tied up in her signature volleyball ponytail and she wore her most prized Mercyhurst volleyball t-shirt, sweatpants, and flip flops. She looked at me, visibly upset.

"Was it not impactful enough for you?" the younger version of myself looked up at me with tears in her eyes. "Because it was for me."

A piece of my heart broke, and my throat tightened. No, no. That's not why I don't tell the whole story. It was definitely impactful—it was the most pivotal experience of my life. It uprooted everything I thought I knew and allowed me to find out who I was underneath all the labels and rules and expectations I had been striving to live up to.

"Well, when you downplay some of it, you downplay all of it," she said.

I hadn't realized how much of a disservice I was doing myself by withholding my story. My thoughts bounced through a stream of memories of all the hospital beds I laid in during the summer of 2007.

Kristin Pierce

"Are you scared to share the whole story?" she asked.

Hmm...I'd never considered that before, I replied as I tapped on my chin. Maybe I am scared. Or maybe, I'm scared to speak up about it at all. So many other cancer and chemo stories were so horrific. I guess, I feel guilty that mine went fairly smoothly.

"Smoothly?" she questioned. "Are you for real?" She cocked her head to one side.

Well, compared to other chemo experiences, yeah. It was three months start to finish. My chemo symptoms were mild compared to the norm. I had mild nausea but didn't vomit at all. I was tired, but that was to be expected. The worst parts were when my blood cells bottomed out and I lost my hair. I suppose, I kept telling myself that it could have been way worse, so I shouldn't complain. Other people have had it way worse.

"But those symptoms still devastated us and broke our heart," she said, seeming confused. "It could have been worse?" she pondered. "Well, we just about died. So, yeah, I guess that would have been worse".

As her honesty hit me in the heart, a lump formed in my throat, and I blinked back the tears that had formed behind my eyes.

"You need to write this—for you, you know. If it transforms other people, that's a perk, but it is meant to transform you," she said as she pointed to her own heart. "It doesn't matter how long it takes. Dig it all up. We are ready," she smiled up at me. "That's why I'm here."

FEAR HAS A PURPOSE

"Whatever you fear most has no power—
it is your fear that has the power."
– Oprah

Fear was an intense theme inside my head. Not always. But when I stretched my comfort zone into the realm of vulnerability, fear showed up with a vengeance. Lately, fear leaked into my thoughts, seeped into my veins, and showed up in my life. Insecurities, doubt, and incessant and limiting self-talk had consumed my mind. I was flared because my ego was scared. There was no escaping it, and that I knew to be true. It was time to sit down with fear and find out what it was here to teach me.

The ego is the part of the mind that mediates between the conscious and subconscious minds. It acts like a helicopter parent in an attempt to protect and keep you safe from harm, humiliation, probable failure, and any other potentially embarrassing occurrences. To do so, it uses the strategies of fear and doubt as control tactics, while reminding you of your deepest fears and insecurities via worst case scenarios and limiting self-talk. And while the ego is often negatively perceived and its methods quite toddler-like, it is only attempting to do its job of keeping you safe.

Fear has a purpose. Actually, all emotions have a purpose. But the purpose of fear is to create activity. It is supposed to make you do something, take action, create action. This can include taking proactive steps, reflecting on the limiting voice you hear inside your head, or reaching out to someone for moral support. When fear is held in, stuffed down or running rampant through the body without an emotional outlet, it piles up and pushes the nervous system into survival mode.

While working through edits on earlier versions of this book, I realized I needed to move my body and get out of my head. After lacing up my shoes, I walked out into the fresh morning air with no phone and no music to distract me. The crisp air filled my nostrils, and I found a peaceful slice of Heaven in the quiet morning around me. The birds chirped and flocks of geese flew overhead, honking in a celebration of glee. The sleepy grass had started showing the slightest hint of green underneath the hibernating brownish hue of winter. Spring was here, and I realized that my heart was ready to stop hibernating in fear. When I returned home, I felt so much lighter. It's amazing how critical movement and nature are for the soul.

The morning sun was inviting me to embrace its warmth, so I packed up my computer and notebook to set up camp on the front step. As I scrolled through my manuscript, I heard my mind remind me, *this is impossible.* I took a deep breath to interrupt the fear that I had grown far too accustomed to hearing while writing this book.

Why am I so scared to let this flow? I wondered.

"Being logical is safer." Was the response that popped into my mind. Left brained and logical is what I was taught to value and trust. Thus, vulnerability, speaking up, and being intuitive was actually quite dangerous. No wonder my ego was flared.

Up next came a laundry list of reasons why I was afraid. Apparently, there was some emotional baggage to unpack before I'd be ready to proceed, so I dove in.

Fear number one. For starters, how egotistical does one have to be to think that a personal memoir matters at all in the midst of a global pandemic, Black Lives Matter movement, and human trafficking awareness? In truth, it doesn't matter in the least.

Fear number two. Next up was the fear of offending people with my perspectives. *Oh, please,* I thought, as I rolled my eyes at myself. Even if I sugar coat and bubble wrap every opinion I share, someone will probably still be offended. And if that offended person shows up in my awareness, it is a mirror for me to work through my own deep-seated fear of rejection. What an opportunity. A quote came to mind by Dita Von Teese, "You can be the ripest, juiciest peach in the world, and there's still going to be someone who hates peaches." But what if you truly (and I mean truly, madly, deeply) love and accept all of your peachy self? Do you still need those situations to arise? I could play the duality game of blame, or I could take ownership of my experience and use the situations that arise in my life as opportunities to heal my inner world.

Fear number three. Being associated with cancer. I do not call myself a "cancer survivor" because I no longer think cancer was something to fight and fear. At the time I was going through the experience, sure, I was in survival mode. But now, I see that cancer was an opportunity to reassess my life and to peel back all of the "BS" beliefs that I'd adopted, without question, to find out who I really was underneath it all. Clearly, there is more work to be unraveled within myself around the word "cancer".

Fear number four. *I have no idea what I'm doing. I don't know how to write a memoir. What if I write about the most life-altering moment of my life and it is completely awful?* My good old ego was always looking out for me like an overprotective helicopter parent. Deep breath.

Once I worked through the laundry list, I could see that my ego was overreacting in an effort to keep me safe. After all, that is the ego's job. Like I said, fear has a purpose. But it was time I stopped letting fear immobilize me and, instead, use it to create activity.

REBIRTH-DAY

"**W**hat's this, Mommy?" Aspen asked, as she picked up a book off my desk.

"Oh, that's a book I was part of a few years ago. I booked a photoshoot to celebrate my ten-year 'rebirth-day' and was asked to be a part of this book."

"What's a 'rebirth-day'?" my son, Kendrix, asked.

"A rebirth-day is kind of like a real birthday. It happens on the same date every year, and it is a celebration—a happy day. Every September 20th, I celebrate my rebirth-day as the day I finished chemotherapy and headed back to college."

"Is that where Daddy was?" Aspen interjected. "At college?"

"Yes, you're right. He was." I could tell they were starting to put the pieces of this story together.

"Was he your boyyyyfriend?" Kendrix asked, and they both giggled.

"No, he wasn't, but I did think he was pretty cute," I winked at them.

"Can you show us the book?" Aspen asked.

I hesitated. This was precisely why I needed to write my memoir—for my kids. I needed to share my experience and the lessons I was still learning from it.

"Well, I don't really want to read this to you," I said.

"Why not?"

"Well, some perspectives of cancer make it seem like it's a really bad, scary thing that we need to hate, fight, and be afraid of. But, it's not. Cancer is what happens when we stop listening to our bodies, don't take care of our whole selves, hold our emotions in, stop paying attention to our hearts, or have a lot of fear that takes over our minds," I told them.

"Yeah, that's why you're supposed to listen when your body talks to you," Kendrix said with a confident nod.

"Mommy, why did you have cancer then?" Aspen asked.

"Well, honey, I had forgotten how to listen to my body. My thoughts were so loud that I just listened to those rather than my body's messages."

"Oh, that's not good," Kendrix said, wide-eyed.

"No, it wasn't. But my body did find a way to get my attention, don't you think?"

"Yeah, I think it did," Aspen agreed, as the gears in her mind visibly spun.

"I think it called you on the phone and said, 'Yoo hoo! Are you listening?!'" Kendrix said, as he made a silly face.

"Will you read us the book if we promise to remember that we don't need to be afraid if we listen to our bodies?" Aspen bargained. "Because we are good at listening to our bodies, right Kendy?"

"Yep," he nodded. "So good."

"Can I think about it?" I asked, as I pulled both of them in for a hug and planted a kiss on each of their foreheads. "Now, let's go have some supper."

September 20th is a big day for me. It is the anniversary of my liberation from the Cancer Centre as I was released back into the wild to pick up the pieces of myself. Every year, I spend my rebirth-day reflecting on that summer and all of the gifts that it has brought to the surface. This is an important ritual to honour how I've grown, what I've learned, I celebrate how my cosmic hammer experience set the wheel of change in motion to help me become the person I am becoming today. It is without a doubt that I know that experience will continue to reveal lessons to me for as long as I live, as long as I continue to pay attention.

For my ten-year rebirth-day, I wanted to celebrate the milestone, so I booked a photo shoot with a talented photographer friend. As we drove out to the find the perfect backdrop of stunning Saskatchewan fields and summertime skies, the photographer mentioned that she had been asked to collaborate with a friend of hers to create a cancer survivor book. "You have to be part of it!" she said, enthusiastically.

Instantly, my guard went up. *I don't know about this,* I thought. Something didn't feel right. The word "survivor" had always rubbed me the wrong way. Once I investigated why, I realized it was because the word "survivor" seemed to keep people in the victim mindset with cancer as the opposition. I knew my perspective of cancer differed greatly from the norm, which could rub people the wrong way. Here I was, already judging my perspective of cancer before I'd even opened my mouth. As an intensely self-critical human, I realized that self-criticism can be a form of self-protection...you know the "I'll judge myself first before anyone else gets a chance" kind of thing. However, once I discovered the root of my fear, I knew that was the exact reason to say "yes". It was time to stop hiding and start speaking up.

We setup camp beside a long gravel road that stretched off into the distance, surrounded by stunning, flowering fields. It was the perfect summer evening as the sun still hung high in the wide-open sky at 7:00 a.m.. I stood in a vibrant yellow canola field in all of its flowering glory, which made a wonderful backdrop for our celebratory shoot. I awkwardly rode a bike in a dress down the gravel road, changed my wardrobe multiple times in the setting sun, and then posed with the picture my college friend had snapped of me ten years prior.

"Okay, I'll do it," I agreed as we drove home from the photoshoot. As hesitant and uncomfortable as I felt, I knew there must be some growth in it for me. In that moment, I vowed to myself that I would not filter my experience to make it fit the understanding of anyone else. I gave myself permission to share my experience through my lens since I was being featured to tell my story anyway.

As the interview date approached for the survivor book, all kinds of fear surfaced—symptoms, dreams, doubt, problems in life—you name it. The interview was stretching me a little too far outside my comfort zone, and my ego was throwing a hissy fit to try to get me to bail. Luckily, this time I understood the internal war and wasn't about to let a creative array of ego excuses get in the way.

When the day finally arrived, my stomach performed flips while I drove to meet the interviewer at a local coffee shop. As I gripped the steering wheel with clammy palms, I noticed my clenched jaw and tense shoulders. Clearly, my mind was wound up about this. "Deep breath, Kristin. You can do this," I whispered to myself as I tried to calm my nerves and lower my shoulders.

A bell jingled on the door as I entered the quaint shop and goosebumps formed on my skin. The aroma of coffee surrounded me and filled my nostrils. Glancing around, looking for a woman sitting alone at a table, a fine sheen of sweat broke out on my forehead. She hadn't arrived yet, so I chose an open table and sat down. The few extra minutes of preparation time allowed me to attempt to calm myself and lower my guard before we dove in.

Every time the coffee shop bell jingled, my eyes darted towards the door. My nerves frayed in anticipation.

Finally, she entered.

"Kristin?" she asked as she approached me.

"Hi! Yes, that's me," I responded as I extended my hand for an introduction. "It's nice to officially meet you."

"Thank you for coming to talk with me," she replied. "Can I get you a drink?"

"Sure," I obliged. We ordered our tasty drinks, making small talk as they were being prepared. With drinks in hand, we sat down and got to it.

Kristin Pierce

Raw and real. No filters, I reminded myself. *She gets the whole story.*

After about 45 minutes of steady question-and-answer, she concluded that she had enough information to put together a write up for the book. We thanked each other and then parted ways. A sigh of relief came out of my mouth as I walked towards my car. As usual, the story in my overactive mind proved far more terrifying than real life.

When the book was published, I felt obligated to buy one; and yet, I found myself feeling incredibly hesitant about it. When I got my hands on a copy, my nerves soared as I reluctantly flipped through until I found the write-up about me. *What is it that bothers me so much about this?* I wondered. As I read through the feature, my ego ever so slowly started to settle. In that moment, I began to realize that fear of speaking against the grain was the root of my emotional trigger.

Of all the stories in the book, mine was the only one that shared the growth, change, and transformation I discovered within the cancer experience, which was exactly why it needed to be in the book to begin with. That was also why my ego was so scared of attending the interview: because I knew my experience would stick out like a sore thumb. In the end, it did and that was okay. Cancer hadn't attacked me. Cancer was the result of many years of storing old wounds and stuffing emotions within myself. It blew up my life to open my mind, my heart, my eyes, and my soul to more healing and self-understanding than I could have ever dreamed of. In that moment, I felt proud that I'd shared my story as bravely as I had, but I still felt nowhere near ready to write about my experience.

"Why is there so much fear around cancer?" I vented to my husband. I felt so frustrated. Not at anyone in particular, but in the fear-based understanding of cancer itself.

"Is it because we are taught to believe that cancer is more powerful than us? Is it because we hand our healing over to the doctors? Is it because we don't realize how much healing power we hold within ourselves? Is it because we believe cancer is our fate? I mean, 'one in four' isn't the greatest 'statistic'," I said, visibly fuming. "But, it's all crap."

"I hate how we are programmed to think we have no power over our health or our mindsets or our fates. It's so frustrating to me. Just go to the doctor, they'll fix you," I said as I rolled my eyes.

"I think you need to share that," my husband mirrored back to me.

"Ughhh," I let out a frustrated sigh. "I'm not ready. It still triggers me too much."

"What's wrong with that?" he prodded. "Anger is supposed to cause movement, right? Isn't that what you'd say to me?"

"Damn you," I replied through my smile, reflecting upon what he said. "Yes, that is what I'd say to you."

"What if we didn't fear cancer? What if we listened to our bodies and our hearts long before it had to get that bad? What if I had listened to my body before it got that bad?"

"Would you have learned any of this?" my husband questioned.

"I don't know. I hope so."

"Then, it had to happen for you. You wouldn't be where you are now without having that experience," he said.

"You're not wrong," I smiled. In that moment, my mind was opened ever so slightly to the possibility of writing about my experience. Yes, my perspective differed, and that spooked my ego. Maybe that's the exact reason why I needed to share it.

What if we didn't get caught up in the victim mindset? What if we changed the narrative? What if we changed the perspective and the understanding of health and healing? What if we asked, "Why did I need to go through that experience? Why did it happen for me? What growth have I found because of it?" Because even the most devastating experiences have a silver lining if you dig deep enough. The understanding may not be visible from the surface and it won't always make sense to the rational mind, but somewhere within, there will be profound lessons waiting to be unwrapped.

A FEAR EPIDEMIC

"The victim mindset dilutes the human potential.
By not accepting personal responsibility for our circumstances,
we greatly reduce our power to change them."
– Steve Maraboli

A ll of the cancer fundraisers and events I attended always framed cancer as something to fight, blame, and fear.

Team names included: Fuck cancer. Cancer sucks. Cancer warriors. And for my first post-cancer fundraiser, our team name was The Neon Cancer Ninjas.

At first, I jumped on the bandwagon. It was hard not to—especially when you want to help but have no idea how to. But as I gained some space and healing from my personal experience, my perspective began to shift. Soon, I began to hear a new narrative—one that didn't sit well with me once I understood the impact that fear has on the body and mind.

The speeches preached:

"Early detection is key."

"Book your annual physical."

"Get genetic testing if cancer runs in your family."

The empowering statistics included, "One in four of all Canadians will have cancer in their lives."

Wait a minute, I thought. *This doesn't feel light.* As I looked around me, it seemed I was the only one shaking my head. This messaging felt so far from empowering and it took me a while to figure out why. Eventually, I realized it felt restricting because the "awareness" being shared was rooted in fear.

I left that last cancer event, the last one I ever attended, with a frown on my face and a tight feeling in my chest. I realized that everyone was blaming cancer for taking their loved ones and preparing to fight when cancer inevitably came knocking on their own door.

This isn't how awareness is supposed to feel, I thought.

There is no doubt that losing loved ones is hard. And cancer can be devastating. I can vouch for that. But the thought that kept echoing through my mind was: This is not how we heal.

This is not how we heal.

This is not how we heal.

This is not how we heal.

We don't heal by fuelling fear and giving away our power to cancer. How is that awareness? It was more like fearmongering cloaked with a fancy charade of "awareness". It didn't feel aligned. It didn't feel how true awareness was meant to feel. That was when I realized that I could no longer submerge myself in that type of a mindset.

True awareness feels expansive. It feels freeing. It creates a sense of empowerment and insight. It's that "aha" moment where you realize something incredible that alters the course of your life. That's the feeling I want to share in this book. True awareness doesn't pass the blame, it brings personal ownership. And ownership of one's experience brings empowerment.

I guess I could call true awareness...self-awareness. To me, self-awareness is about becoming more aware of your mind, body, emotions, heart, and inner self. It is about connecting with yourself so you can trust and honour your feelings, rather than ignore and stuff them deep down inside. It involves learning to listen to your internal cues (the messages from your body), catching

15

your internal self-talk, and honouring your heart's desires. Self-awareness means looking deeper into the meaning beneath the symptoms, illness, or disease that shows up for us.

I quickly realized that "cancer awareness" was not synonymous with personal growth or self-awareness, which I felt were the true keys to healing—and that didn't feel right for me. In hindsight, I can see that the reason those events didn't feel aligned was because they contributed to the fear epidemic around cancer—which actually feeds cancer and illness, rather than heals it. Fear breeds more fear. Fear triggers survival mode. And long-term fear debilitates the immune system.

How backwards is that?

Cancer is something that we have been conditioned to fear. For some, cancer is seen as a death sentence. We are taught to expect it. If it runs in your family, then cancer is guaranteed to knock on your door. But does this have to be true? What if we stopped expecting it? What can we do differently?

FEAR FEEDS CANCER

"Fear does not stop death, it stops life."
– Vi Keeland

The mind is the most powerful influencer over how you experience and create your life. When harnessed, it can create the most incredible, mind-blowing advancements and opportunities known to man. When infected by fear, perceived stress, and limiting beliefs, it can become as destructive and unpredictable as a natural disaster.

What does this have to do with fear and cancer?

Fear feeds cancer.

Fear feeds cancer. And not just cancer, it feeds all kinds of illnesses and diseases. When the body goes into fear mode, its main concern is survival. The nervous system has two modes of operation: survival mode, commonly known as "fight or flight", and healing mode, commonly known as "rest and digest".

When danger arises or when the mind is taken over by fear, it creates an insurgent wave that starts a domino effect within the body. Physically, the amygdala—the part of the limbic brain that controls the body's fight or flight response—kicks into high gear, triggering a stress response that moves throughout the body at breakneck speed. The body shifts into survival mode, releasing stress hormones into the blood stream, which direct blood flow away from the torso and into the appendages in case you need to fight, run, freeze, or faint as a survival tactic to escape imminent danger. Due to decreased blood flow to the abdomen, digestion slows, immune function is suppressed, lymphatic function decreases, and sleep is often affected—because obviously, sleep isn't a priority when in danger. The nervous system is built to kick into survival mode when danger arises, and then reset itself to rest and digest mode once the coast is clear. At that point, our digestion turns back on, blood flow returns to the body's core, immune function is restored, and mental and emotional processing begins.

Our bodies are not equipped to function in emergency mode long-term. The nervous system is built to kick into action when danger arises, and then it resets itself to rest and digest mode once the coast is clear. At that point, our digestion turns back on, blood flow returns to the body's core, immune function is restored, and mental and emotional processing begins. So, when bombarded with fear of illness, cancer "awareness" commercials, posters in the doctor's office, and other forms of fearmongering that are meant to inform us, but only do a fine job of feeding fear, it puts the body into fight or flight mode and creates the perfect internal environment for illness to thrive.

Although society has evolved from the days of the caveman, we still face the stress of survival, it just comes in different forms now—technology, bills, childcare, extracurricular activities, social media, overbooked schedules, prolonged screen time, sedentary lifestyles, keeping up with the Joneses, fear of illness, etc. When you meet a bear in the woods, when you need to jump out of the way of an oncoming bus, or when your main source of income collapses and you need to figure out how to feed your family, these survival responses are obviously helpful. And it is not news that the body and mind need to rest, digest, and heal in order to stay healthy. It becomes a problem when survival mode is a long-term state-of-being instead of a temporary survival mechanism because stress and healing cannot coexist. The bodymind, a holistic term for the interconnectedness between body and mind, cannot heal when it is in stress mode. It is either in fight or flight mode or it is in rest and digest. There is no in between.

You can see how this becomes a slippery slope into digestive problems, chronic suppressed immune issues, lymphatic backup, chronic fatigue, and chronic sleep problems, to name a few. Not to mention the effects of the stress itself on the mind and body. None of what I say is to undermine the importance of the functions of our nervous system, but rather to show that living in a state of long-term stress is detrimental to the body, which is not helpful for anyone's state of health in the case of a pandemic sweeping through the world—whether that pandemic be cancer, economic collapse, heart disease, or COVID-19.

Stress can exist on a daily basis if we choose it—but, it is most definitely a choice. You get to choose what information, people, resources, and media you engage with. Stress levels can be greatly impacted by our personal perspective, state of mind, and how we take care of ourselves in mind, body, and spirit. If you don't believe me, try ramping up your self-care, mindset work, exercise, and self-reflection practices for two weeks, then see how you feel.

Over time, I've come to gain a different perspective of fear. While I'm sure I let fear drive my actions for more of my lifetime than I'd like to admit, I now see fear as something to lean into rather than run away from. Fear arises when we move out of our comfort zones, challenge our perceived limits, and go against the grain of what we have been conditioned to believe. Fear is not something to try to escape from. On the contrary, fear is a gift to be unraveled and a clue to be investigated, because it is always rooted in a "story" that is contrived in the mind. Due to this shift in perspective, it has allowed me to investigate and unravel the fear that kept me from sharing my story for so long.

LUCKY THIRTEEN

"An awareness of one's mortality can lead you to wake up
and live an authentic, meaningful life."
– Bernie Siegel, M.D.

Thirteen is a lucky number in my family. I was born on the thirteenth of March, and my twin brothers, Kenton and Kiel, joined the "Lucky Thirteen Birthday Club" just fifteen months later. Friday the Thirteenths became my favourite birthdays, and we referred to "Lucky Thirteen" as our special number, instead of buying into superstition. Since then, my daughter was also born on the thirteenth. So how fitting when I finally realized after writing the majority of this book, that this year would be thirteen years since my summer of cancer.

It is hard to believe that thirteen years have passed since I had cancer.

Thinking back to myself as a twenty-one-year-old cancer patient, at the time, I wasn't able to digest the questions that raced through my mind and the understanding I craved. Mainly, *How could such a catastrophic health event happen to someone so physically healthy?*

To better portray this evolution, let me paint a picture of the young woman I was before cancer. I was a headstrong, very left-brained, athletic girl that was determined and stubborn. I was extremely logical, rational, judgmental, and intellectual. As an elite athlete, with an academic and athletic volleyball scholarship to study sports medicine, I juggled high grades, daily practices, home games, team road trips, and workouts, with a touch of social life mixed in. I had outrageous expectations for myself and was intensely self-critical; but I was driven. I pushed my body to extremes, thinking "no pain, no gain." Mind over matter, right?

I didn't understand how poorly I was treating myself. I took care of myself in the physical realm, eating healthy and exercising, almost to a fault. Speaking of faults, I focused on those a lot. I believed in what I could see—the physical and tangible. I believed emotions equated to weakness, so I stuffed them deep within myself. I was so disconnected from the mental and emotional aspects of myself that I didn't notice the red flags and the caution signs along the way. I was in need of an intense wake-up call, and that is exactly what I got.

The lessons and realizations that have been revealed over the past thirteen years have served as stepping stones to prepare my heart, mind, and soul for sharing this story. I have rumbled over and over again with the experience, my understanding of health, life and how the world works, the aha moments that have come forth, and how an experience with cancer has wholly changed who I am and who I think I need to be. The more I unwrap, the more fully I become my true self.

Writing this book was definitely not easy, but it was entirely worth it. Every rumbling that came forth allowed me to question my understanding, unravel limiting beliefs I learned along the way, lean into my knowing, and plant my feet more firmly in myself. Though I didn't realize it at the time of embarking on this writing journey, the synchronicity of Lucky Thirteen was working its subconscious magic all along.

As I finished writing the chapter, the creaking of the stairs grabbed my attention. "What are you doing, Mommy?" I spun in my chair to find my daughter wrapped up in her blanket at the bottom of the stairs, squinting from the early morning light.

"Good morning, sweetie. I'm working on my memoir," I replied.

"What's a memoir?" she asked, rubbing her sleepy eyes as she walked towards me and climbed onto my lap.

"It's a story about a part of someone's life."

"What part of your life are you writing about?" she asked. "About when you were white?"

She was referring to a black and white picture of me hung on our master bedroom wall from 2007. My friend, Ang, begged me to be her subject for her photography class project after I had returned to college post-chemotherapy. At the time I reluctantly agreed, but now I'm so grateful for her persistence.

"Yes, honey. That's what I'm writing about."

"Oh," she said, and I could see her wheels turning, thinking of how to phrase her next question. In many ways, she was just like me as a child. But in more ways, I was amazed by her intuitive nature and her willingness to speak any and all truths, observations, and questions that dropped into her mind. I had a pretty good feeling I used to be just like her.

As I observed her with reverence, she broke our pondering silence. "What are you going to call your book?"

"I'm going to call it My Cosmic Hammer," I smiled, knowing full well what was coming next.

She tipped her head to one side and said, "What's a 'Cosmic Hammer'?"

COSMIC HAMMERS

"I had to make you uncomfortable,
otherwise you never would have moved."
– The Universe

"A cosmic hammer is when something happens that changes your whole life. It is a life-altering event that shakes up every part of you—your mind, heart, life, and soul—and helps you reflect upon what you really want for your life, how you want to live it, and who you want to be."

"Would that be like when Great Kate died?" Aspen asked. Great Kate was my grandma and Aspen's great grandma. I'd only ever referred to her as "Grandma Katie" until my daughter was born. When the great grandkids came along, Grandma's rhyming nickname rolled off the tongue much smoother for the little ones and ended up sticking like glue.

"Sure, sweetie. When loved ones pass away, that can be a cosmic hammer. Anytime something major happens that makes you reassess your life, that's a cosmic hammer."

"What about when the virus came, and all the schools closed, and we had to stay home?"

She was referring to the global pandemic ravaging 2020, which had created upheaval in her own little world, helping her relate to our conversation. "Yes. That's a pretty big cosmic hammer for the whole world, wouldn't you say?"

"Yeah, that's a big one. I also think cosmic hammers are when people get sick. It's like their bodies are trying to say, 'Helloooo?! It's time to listen to me now!'"

"You've got it, sweetie. There are a lot of different ways that cosmic hammers can show up—sometimes they are big, sometimes they are small—but they are always happening for us; to help us learn and grow. I think cosmic hammers come to help us see something in a new way, to open our minds, to help us shift how we think, and to get us back in alignment with ourselves. When we open our minds, we also open our hearts, and that's where all the magic happens. When we have open hearts, we make choices that feel right for us, we are connected with our bodies, and we trust our inner knowing."

"Why would anyone close their heart?" she asked, bewildered.

I paused, amazed by the things that kids pick up on. "Hmm...well you know how you feel when your tummy gets sore and you feel scared that you might throw up?"

"Mmhmm," she nodded as she crinkled her nose.

"And you know how you curl up with your legs pulled in towards your chest?"

"Yeah."

"Well, that's how you are protecting yourself when you don't feel good. When people feel scared, we tend to close our hearts as a way to protect ourselves. It doesn't mean that it works, but it happens a lot. Anyways, when you close your heart, it is harder to listen to yourself, your body, and your intuition. But when you open your heart, you can be connected with it and stay true to yourself. Kids are really good at having open hearts."

"Yeah, I'm good at having an open heart," she nodded, proudly. "And I'm good at drawing."

"You sure are," I agreed, as I squeezed her extra tight and kissed her on the forehead.

"Did you hear that, Momma? My tummy just growled," she said, astonished.

"Well, what did it have to say?" I asked.

She cocked her head and gazed upward as if she was listening. "What was that, body?" she whispered, then turned her head toward me. "It said it wants porridge for breakfast."

"Way to listen to your body, girly," I said. "What if we all knew that our bodies are always talking to us to try to help us?"

"Well, they are. Our bodies are smart."

"And what if we all knew that everything in life, even the cosmic hammers, happens to help us grow and learn? Wouldn't that be pretty powerful?"

"I think life is way easier when we know that," she replied.

"You're a wise one, girlfriend," I told her.

"I know," she beamed, then hopped off my lap and ran upstairs for breakfast. I jotted down a few notes on my notepad, amazed at the perspective children can impart just by being themselves.

While cosmic hammers can be painful experiences, they are an opportunity to crack wide open, peel back all the layers, and let the light in. Life-altering events are *supposed* to alter your life. They are *supposed* to shake you up. They are *supposed* to make you question everything you think you know. When life brings you to your knees—shattered and in shambles—it is an incredible opportunity to reassess everything you think you are and have been taught you have to be. This moment can be an awakening if you so choose it. The journey to unbecome all that you are not is one that will forever transform your life. This is the story of my cosmic hammer.

PART TWO:

My Cosmic Hammer

""Not all storms come to disrupt your life.
Some come to clear a path."
– Unknown

MISS INDEPENDENT

I grew up in the small, rural town of Rosetown, Saskatchewan, Canada, in the middle of the stereotypical Saskatchewan prairies where the old saying goes, "you can watch your dog run away for three days". The landscape was incredibly flat with highways that stretched straight out into the distance for miles on end. Fields of crops lined the highways and created the look of a quilted blanket when viewed from above. Rosetown was a safe, small town, and a nice place to raise a family. With a population of about 2,500, it was a place where everyone knew each other and, like most small towns, news spread as fast there as it does on social media.

When I was 15 months old, I became a big sister to two identical twin boys, Kenton and Kiel. In the blink of an eye, I dropped my position as "baby" of the family and was promoted to big sister. I was totally smitten with my brothers and could often be found dancing or entertaining them as they sat side-by-side in their bouncy chairs. I took pride in doing things for myself and being a great helper for my mom as she juggled us three babes in diapers.

My brothers and I were built-in buddies when we were young. I was so proud to tell everyone that I had twin brothers, and I took my role as big sister very seriously. Our fun adventures were peppered with the typical sibling fights and more than a few mischievious incidents. One of our less brilliant ideas resulted in me agreeing to test drive a laundry hamper down the stairs that my brothers had pushed from the top. What started with good intent, resulted in the laundry hamper catching on the first step and me tumbling the entire way down the stairs and ending with a muffled cry at the bottom of the stairs from underneath the hamper. Luckily, the stairs were carpeted and no blood resulted. As we grew up, we spent many hours together building with Lego, jumping on the trampoline, building forts with couch cushions, playing mini sticks, Nintendo, tag, and the list goes on.

The closeness in age with my brothers sometimes created a sense of rivalry between us. I butted heads the most with my youngest brother, Kiel, since we were both headstrong and so much alike. The oldest of the twins, Kenton, quickly became the mediator between us. Often, I felt the need to remind my brothers of our birth order and my superiority—that was, until they grew bigger than me and I knew to leave well enough alone. As we grew up, our conflicts turned into a battle of wits, words, and insults. Yet in spite of our sibling spats, I would have done anything to protect my brothers.

My parents were supportive, ambitious, hard-working business owners who would do anything for their kids. My dad worked sixty hours a week, while my mom worked and ran the household. Dad was a strong, muscular, determined man who oozed sarcasm, practicality, and common sense. He loved hunting and the great outdoors. Mom was a smart, productive, and practical woman who could schedule our busy lives like a game of Tetris, fitting in necessary appointments with our activities, events, and social lives. She could organize her way out of any disaster, was sharp as a tack, and never let a detail slip passed her. My parents instilled in us a strong work ethic, an ambitious drive, and high personal standards.

Many fond memories fill my mind of a pretty great childhood. In the winters, we were lucky to attend annual ski trips to the Rocky Mountains of Alberta and British Columbia, which created a family bond and memories that would last a lifetime. In the summers, we took to our camper for lake adventures, playground games, and beach days until my parents chose a permanent location to build a cabin. Christmases were divided between my grandparents' houses. Birthday parties were attended by cousins and grandparents, who all lived nearby. Friends were plentiful and family friend Friday nights were always something to look forward to.

My Cosmic Hammer

I was a strong-willed little girl with a mind of my own and a gentle, empathetic heart. I was extremely observant and aware of my surroundings and how other people were feeling, which I never equated to being intuitive until well into my adult years. Being naturally athletic, I enjoyed being active and trying many different sports and activities throughout my childhood years.

As I grew up, my strong mind began to shine through, which often became the root of the spats with my brothers and the conflict with my mom. I poked holes through explanations that didn't make logical sense. Over time, I began to value being smart and logical as the safe way to exist in the world, while seeing emotional expression as a sign of weakness. I took pride having a solid, logical head on my shoulders, which had no space for emotions. Instead, I kept my thoughts and emotions tucked nicely inside myself for safe keeping. When I did cry, it was often due to physical injury and everyone knew my tears meant something serious.

As a teen, I was expected to take responsibility for myself, my schoolwork, my academic preparations, and my decisions, which I believe set me up for success. My parents had high academic expectations, and I began to apply those high expectations to every arena of my life, putting pressure on myself to be responsible, succeed, and avoid making mistakes. Praise and encouragement for being "smart", "strong", "capable" and "independent" built a belief within me that I could figure out and accomplish anything I set my mind to. However, I also began to believe that those labels were who had to be all of the time, rather than just an expression of the many facets of my behaviour. Wearing the mask of "Miss Independent", I eventually found myself hesitating to ask questions, ask for help, or to share my feelings, deep ponderings, and the pangs of my soul. It felt safer to keep it in and attempt to figure it all out on my own.

As I'm sure you can see, a theme emerged about rejecting my emotions and treasuring my logical mind. While my strong mind helped me in more ways than I can count and took me far in athletics, it also allowed logic to shut down my intuitive feelings, disregard my emotions, and create intense negative self-talk whenever I didn't live up to the "smart", "strong", and "independent"

labels I had created for myself.

MENTAL TOUGHNESS

When high school came along, my schedule quickly filled to the brim with sports. Eventually, I had to make a choice; be decent at all of the sports I played or specialize in only a couple. In the end, it came down to track and field and volleyball. I loved track and field with my whole heart, so I knew I couldn't give it up; and volleyball was my passion. I decided to do both.

There was nothing I didn't like about volleyball. It was competitive, intense, and I always gave 110%. I could be found diving all over the court to dig a ball, swinging hard and smart with every ball the setter sent my way, and grunting with every burst of energy. I loved everything about the sport. I went all in, and I was fortunate to have incredible coaches that encouraged and believed in me, helping me reach my potential and become the best athlete I could be.

Throughout my high school years, my commitment to volleyball became as intense as my schedule. Practices, games, and tournaments consumed almost every weekend from grade nine to twelve. I played high school volleyball, club volleyball, and provincial team volleyball, while also fitting in year-round track and field practices, provincial team track, and track meets. Mix in homework, studying, weightlifting, family, and a minimalist social life—I learned early on how to fit the pieces together like a jigsaw puzzle. My annual calendar soon began to resemble a full-time job.

With a jam-packed schedule, the temptations of a teenage girl often grabbed hold of my mind. Missing out on parties, social events, and friend time sometimes made me feel that I was sacrificing too much for volleyball. At times I felt like I had no life, when in reality, volleyball created incredible travel opportunities, life-long friendships, and dreams that became my vehicle to a full ride scholarship. It was a huge commitment, but I loved the sport and the opportunities that came with it.

Being immersed in elite athletics for much of my middle school and high school years was an experience that had a huge impact on the development of my character, confidence, and mindset. Early on, I began to learn how emotions could be used in a positive way to pump me up, or how my thoughts, fears, and worries could get in my head and negatively impact my athletic performance. Strong, steady minds were always praised and valued, while emotions seemed to wreak havoc; further solidifying my perceived "understanding" of self.

Athletics taught me about strength training, mental toughness, what foods to eat to fuel peak performance, and how to push myself to be the best athlete I could be. From full on mental toughness seminars to guided visualizations, we were taught to not let our heads get in the way of our performance. This meant having a tough mindset, not letting emotions affect us, and staying focused on competing with ourselves to improve our skills. I realized quite quickly that if I let my limiting thoughts and emotions run me, my athletic performance would suffer and I'd get pulled from the lineup. While I see these learnings as mostly positive, that athletic mindset instilled many beliefs that solidified pushing through pain, that the mind knew better than the body, and that the body was to be strong-armed in order to grow, improve, and succeed.

Not knowing how to deal with my thoughts and emotions, I continued to stuff them down and attempted to mask them by "staying positive". I did not understand that having and expressing emotions was normal and healthy; but rather, thought I needed to reject them at all costs. Thus, I had absolutely no idea what to do with my emotions when they did surface, let alone how to process them. My mind continued to equate emotions with weakness and instability, so whenever I felt them, I buried them deep within myself where they piled up even higher.

FULL RIDE

"Dreams and dedication are a powerful combination."
– William Longgood

One Saturday evening, after a gruelling day of two practices, my club volleyball team gathered on the bleachers to watch a University of Saskatchewan Huskies volleyball game. As I watched the incredible athleticism of the Huskies volleyball players, my jaw dropped in awe. "Wow. I want to do that," rippled through my mind with complete clarity. Instantly, I knew that I wanted to go on to play collegiate level volleyball. With starry eyes, I admired the athletes I dreamed of one day becoming as I overheard my teammates discuss players who had accepted volleyball scholarships to the States. *Whoa.* I was starstruck. Immediately, my dream of earning an athletic scholarship to a university in the States consumed my goals and fuelled my ambitious drive.

It felt like a once-in-a-lifetime opportunity, and I wanted the full meal deal. I didn't want to go to university close to home and rush home every chance I got. That worked for some people, but it wasn't for me. I wanted to launch myself into the immersive university experience someplace far, far away. Why? Well, I guess I wanted to do something different. I wanted to blaze my own trail and that meant having enough space from everything familiar so I could discover who I was. To me, that meant getting way outside my comfort zone.

By the time I'd made it to grade twelve, I was beyond ready to break free of the chains of high school. After getting a taste of the travel and adventure that volleyball had offered, I was ready for a big change. I had worked my butt off and was chomping at the bit to follow my finally unbridled heart.

Since I wanted the immersive experience, I knew I needed to be far enough away that I couldn't sabotage my commitment to myself. My rule of thumb when choosing a school was that it needed to be further than one day's driving distance from home. I'm crazy like that—I'd hop in a car and drive eight hours to get home if I wanted to—and I wasn't about to allow myself to get in my own way. I was ready to launch myself far out of the nest. New friends, new team, new coaches, new teachers all at a new school, in a new city, in a new country. I wanted it all, and I knew it would be epic.

In the end, I received scholarship offers from three schools—Jamestown, North Dakota; Fairbanks, Alaska; and Erie, Pennsylvania.

I decided to study kinesiology. Since I was focused so heavily in athletics, injuries had always popped up. I was very science-focused, had a strong logical mind, and believed in the tangible. Since chemistry, biology, and math were my forte, it made sense for me to follow a science route. I was fascinated by the body. And how in the world are you supposed to know what you want to do with your life at eighteen years old? Sports was all I knew at the time, so I played it safe and stayed in my lane.

My dad was very adamant about guiding my brothers and me to choose a viable profession. In all honesty, the temperaments, work ethic, and determination of his children should have been enough to curb his fear, but instead, the job choice needed to be a logically lucrative one.

As I reviewed the schooling options for the three offers, I also had other major thoughts cross my mind. Jamestown was only an eight-hour drive. Too close, I thought. Alaska? No way. "I don't know if I could handle the cold or that much darkness in the winter months," I said to my parents. We had limited sunlight in Saskatchewan in the winter and I couldn't imagine living in a place with less.

"What about this Erie place? Where is that?" I asked my parents. We looked up Erie on the map and it appeared to be directly between Cleveland, Ohio, Buffalo, and New York. Interesting, I thought. Next, I looked at the map of Pennsylvania. Erie was on the tiny piece of Pennsylvania that touched the

Great Lake of Lake Erie. Pittsburgh was a two-hour drive straight south. After cruising through the details and checking out the website for Mercyhurst, I decided I wanted to explore it.

After one visit down to Erie, with its stunning campus filled with flowers, the magnificent brick architecture, and its small class sizes, I was captivated. Mercyhurst was a private catholic school, nestled on a hill. The character of the buildings made campus feel regal and refined. The school boasted twenty-seven athletic teams from the typical sports like football, ice hockey, volleyball, basketball, soccer, wrestling, lacrosse, and baseball, to the less common ones like rowing, water polo, field hockey, tennis, and more. I was so impressed when the campus guide shared the statistic of the number of athletes on campus from all over the world.

One of my best friends from my club volleyball team, Christine, and another fellow Team Saskatchewan teammate, Sara, also received scholarship offers to Mercyhurst. On the visit, we were invited to practice and stay overnight with our potential teammates. While the coach was intense and intimidating, the team seemed warm and welcoming. I was instantly sold. It already felt like home.

THREE-A-DAYS

"Your body can stand almost anything.
It's your mind you have to convince."
– Unknown

When I first arrived at Mercyhurst for preseason training, I knew it was
going to be intense. Our coach expected a lot and had us dive right into
three-a-day practices in the humid, non-air-conditioned campus gym. For
three weeks in August, we ate, lived, and breathed volleyball in preparation
for our season ahead.

Our days were consumed by intense drills, shuttle sprints, weightlifting, timed
runs, repetitive serving, passing, digging, blocking, hitting, and everything
in between. You have to truly love a sport to endure being put through the
ringer day in and day out without throwing in the towel. Blisters, bruises, and
incredibly sore muscles were an expectation, while ice packs, athletic trainer
support, and appendages supported with athletic tape became part of the
daily routine. Sweatpants, sweaty sports bras, ponytails, and sandals became
a constant wardrobe and nap time became an essential battery recharge
required to make it through the day. My mindset, confidence, and skill set
were tested, stretched, and grown in those intense three weeks that started out
every new volleyball season. Never in my life have I sweat so much in a day.

When I started as a freshman on the team, any confidence I had built up from
previous years seemed to vanish in my new role at the bottom of the totem
pole. I worked my butt off in an attempt to earn a spot on the court and worked

hard on my mental game so as to not be derailed by intimidation.

Having a team to fall into was a helpful transition into college life, especially upon moving to a new country. Considering that every weekend from August to November was full of volleyball games and road trips, my team quickly became family. We ate together, iced our sore muscles together, practiced together, and some of us even lived together. We played games on the bus, laughed our faces off, made memories, and ran lines together until we were on the verge of chucking our guts. To be part of a team meant an immediate sense of belonging in the midst of large-scale change.

Campus life was pretty spectacular. It reminded me of college life in the movies, but instead of fraternities and sororities, we had sports teams. We ate at the cafeteria, lived on campus, walked to and from class, and frequented the gym on a daily basis. Class sizes were small, typically thirty to forty people, which was made possible by the expensive price tag to attend. I managed to juggle daily practices and weight-lifting workouts with classes, schoolwork, and road trips as I adapted to find a new normal. While being the new kid on campus felt incredibly intimidating at first, over time I formed new friendships, found my footing, and began to feel comfortable in my new surroundings.

As I learned about all-things-sports-medicine, my logical brain was in Heaven. From exercise science to nutrition, injury treatment to metabolism, everything I learned I used to create more rigid rules for myself about exercise and food in order to become the best athlete I could be. In hindsight, I can see this learning added to the construction of my tight mental box of conditions that I continually forced myself to meet. Eat this. Don't eat that. Workout every day. Be a better athlete. Mind over matter. Push harder. No pain, no gain. Don't show weakness. Emotions are stupid. When I didn't live within my stiff expectations of self, I drowned myself in guilt, negative self-talk, and self-punishment in the form of extra workouts and limited food intake. While many athletes would agree that there is nothing wrong with this picture, in hindsight, I truly beg to differ. My understanding of health, athletics, and improving as an athlete continued to push me further and further away from my inner wisdom and the messages from my body.

BEER CART GIRL + PRO SHOP BOY

After my first year of college, I took a job at the golf course clubhouse at the lake as the beer cart girl and a server. It was the perfect situation because I could make good tip money, live at the lake, and have plenty of time to fit in my workouts before I had to return to Mercyhurst for preseason in early August. It turned out to be a pretty great job that taught me about golf etiquette, memorizing the regulars' favourite drink orders, and making friendly small talk with strangers. It's also where I met Mark.

My relationship history had been pretty sparse up until that point. My "Miss Independent" demeanor wasn't conducive to needing to be in a relationship, and I was just fine with that. But when Mark came into the picture, I was intrigued. He worked in the pro shop and had his eye on me as soon as I started. We began hanging out as a group with the other clubhouse employees and a romance soon blossomed.

Mark treated me with respect and kindness, and was always making me laugh with his jokes, pranks, and goofy personality. He was committed and open, while I was standoffish and reserved. It was quite foreign for me to be treated with such affection, so I remained hesitant and cautious until he melted my fears and broke down the walls of protection around my heart.

His parents welcomed me with kind hearts and open arms, and while I expected my own parents to be overprotective, it didn't take him long to capture a permanent place in their hearts with his charm, humour, and wit.

With a skeptical view of relationships, I never expected it to last longer than the summer. However, when it was time for me to go back to school, he was adamant on making it work. Mark's perspective of relationships and experience with long-term commitment slowly but surely began to break down some of my mental walls and opened me up to a new possibility. While a long-distance relationship was the last thing I thought I wanted, he opened my mind and my heart to giving it a shot.

For almost two years, we dated long distance while I was at school in Erie, Pennsylvania and he was at home in Saskatchewan, Canada—a thirty-hour drive apart. We spent our summers together and saw each other every few months throughout the school year, while spending hours on the phone in between. We grew very close, as did our families. Our visits throughout the year always seemed to be full of fun adventures, but every so often my reservations popped back up.

MY BODY WHISPERED

"You will never be able to escape from your heart.
So, it is better to listen to what it has to say."
– Paulo Coelho, The Alchemist

In February 2007, I woke up to the beauty and warmth of the tropical sunshine in the Mayan Riviera of Mexico. I was there with Mark and his family for his sister's wedding. It was my first time to Mexico, and I was excited. Eager to take full advantage of my break from the snow flurries that had consumed my third Erie winter, I got up to go for a run and soak up the quiet of the morning. As I pushed off for the first stride of my run, I felt a twang of pain stab me in my lower abdomen, I stopped to investigate. I poked around my abdomen and found that it was tender to the touch. Being the logical sports medicine student and athlete that I was, I chalked it up to the fact that I hadn't warmed up enough, so I stretched out my hip flexors and was forced to take it easy for the rest of my jog.

When I got back to the room, I mentioned the stabbing pain to Mark, but I tried to brush it off as he voiced his concern. It was his sister's wedding after all, and I didn't want to make a fuss. But while I'd swallowed worse pain before, a worried feeling began to niggle in the back of my mind. Something wasn't right. And as I attempted to push the feeling away, it only seemed to grow louder.

When I finally got real with myself, I realized how inauthentic I felt being in Mexico. I had already been questioning my relationship with him for more than a few months but was sticking it out and wearing a smile against the better judgment of my heart. With the wedding vibes in full force, I felt myself leaning away from love while everyone else leaned in.

I had initially brought up my discontent a few months prior, and we went on a "break" for a few weeks—but eventually, I caved into the path of least resistance. It just seemed easier to not break up before I would be home for Christmas. "Make it through the holidays," I told myself. But then the holidays turned into, "Make it through his sister's wedding," since it was already booked. But still, something just didn't feel right. It broke my heart to even think about it, so I tried to convince myself otherwise and focused on the facts: He was a wonderful guy; he treated me like gold; he was hilarious, fun, and always up for an adventure. And most importantly, he had done nothing wrong. Yet, it just didn't *feel* right. And while that should have been enough of a reason to listen to my heart, logic always trumped feelings.

While the week away in the sunshine was a nice escape from school, being in Mexico felt wrong and I was beating myself up for being there. The guilt was heavy, and my guard was up.

The bride and groom were married on the beach surrounded by friends and family. The weather was perfect, and it was a beautiful day full of love and commitment. Mark and his brother stood up as bridesmen for his sister and taking in the wedding festivities made me imagine my own wedding. The problem was, there remained an anxious nudge I kept feeling in my chest. Somewhere deep inside, I knew Mark wasn't the one for me, even if I was terrified to admit it.

My internal knowing was undeniable when people started commenting, "You're next!" to Mark and me. He would light up with a great big smile, and I would force a hesitant smile to hide the fact that a mild panic attack was racing through my body on the inside. I finally got to the point where I could no longer fake that my heart was happy so, instead, I blamed my withdrawn behaviour on the discomfort within my abdomen. I retreated inside myself as I was overcome with the impending doom of hurting Mark and his wonderful family when I'd inevitably break up with him. While the knowing became undeniable, I couldn't bring myself to find the courage to voice my truth. When the week was over, I flew back to Erie, still unsure of how to proceed.

Now, none of what I say is to blame my symptoms on Mark. Not in the least. The moment in Mexico was simply the tipping point. It was when the emotional pileup that I perpetually stuffed back down inside myself could no longer be contained within the walls of my body. It was so much less about the specific situation, and so much more about not being able to hold all of my emotions inside myself anymore. Something had to give.

Eventually, I realized that romance hadn't been the only area of my life where I had been doing what I thought was expected of me instead of listening to my heart. My emotions had been stockpiling over the years. I had always been determined to live up to the expectations of my parents, grandparents, coaches, teachers, and myself—which were often contrived assumptions of what I *thought* was expected of me. Of course, my body tried to get my attention, but my standard response was to disregard, ignore, and press on. And thus, my symptoms continued to grow until I was finally ready to take a look in the mirror.

Over Easter, I took a road trip up to Ontario, Canada to see one of my guy friends from high school. It may have been the hangover, but when I finally opened up about how I felt in my relationship, everything came spilling out. Morgan had a good listening ear, and his honesty helped me realize that what I already knew in my heart was actually worthy of honouring.

"If you're not happy, why would you stay?" Morgan asked, confused, as if it was a no-brainer.

"Because he didn't do anything wrong. I feel like I don't have a valid reason to break up with him. He's such a great guy."

"Your own happiness isn't enough of a reason?" he queried with a frown.

I had so much resistance to seeing the truth of how I felt. To my logical mind, wanting to break up didn't make any sense, so I discounted my unhappiness. Mark checked all the boxes and treated me like gold—which was hard to accept at first—but I could feel in my heart and I knew in my gut that something was missing.

When I returned from my Easter road trip, I couldn't shake the awful feeling in the pit of my stomach. I knew the feeling would not subside until I listened to my heart and spoke my truth. Six weeks of school remained before I would embark on the thirty-hour drive home for the summer. But I had awoken an awareness within myself that was too big to stuff back down. It felt as though I might vomit.

I mustered every ounce of courage in my body as I dialled his number to break up over the phone. It was one of the most heart-breaking experiences I'd ever endured. As I sat cross-legged at my desk, I hung up the phone and looked down to see a puddle of tears had stained the seat of my chair. I felt completely shattered. Not only had I crushed him, but I also knew I was about to crush our families too. Maybe it was all more dramatic in my mind, but that was how I felt. I doubted myself and my truth, wondering if I had made a mistake; but, it was the tiny glimmer of relief that surfaced in my chest that showed me otherwise.

It was so hard to listen to my heart, because there wasn't a logical explanation to back my feeling up. I had learned that every decision needed to be logical, which made honouring my heart almost impossible. Because I had never learned to trust my intuition or my heart, honouring my feelings felt very selfish, cruel, and irrational.

To my surprise, the world didn't end, which was a pretty good lesson in itself: The world doesn't end because you honour your feelings, even when you think it might. The guilt, grief, and sadness took a while to subside, and the fear of seeing his family in the summer reared its ugly head on the regular. But that sliver of relief that I felt, I realized much later that was what alignment felt like—expansion, spaciousness, a glimmer of hope even in the midst of heartbreak.

The experience needed to be big and dramatic because I had been ignoring my heart for too long. I had pushed my inner knowing down for too long, discounting its validity, and eventually I couldn't hold it in any longer.

CAMPUS DOCTOR

When spring arrived, I enjoyed many outdoor runs through the residential streets around campus, trying to process my emotions while taking in the glorious sights and smells of cherry blossoms in bloom. However, I began to notice digestive issues show up with a general feeling of being bloated and "backed up". It was mild, but unusual for me. Eventually, my discomfort grew to the point where I had to go for a run if I hoped to have any kind of release that day. Something was up, so I booked an appointment to see the campus doctor. After a pelvic exam and a series of questions, the doctor told me there was nothing to worry about—it was just constipation. He noted that I could try eating more fibre to help move things along.

"Hmm...okay," I said, hesitantly. "I thought I ate enough fibre, but I guess I could give it a shot."

The next month, my symptoms had progressed. By this time, I had noticed that I could feel a firm area in my lower abdomen. It was hard to feel unless I laid on my back with my legs flat. So, I went back for another doctor's appointment at the campus clinic. This time, after an exam with a different doctor, I was given the same diagnosis, "You're just constipated. Try eating more fibre."

"That's what the last doctor told me; but I already eat a lot of fibre," I protested, feeling confused. They didn't know what else to tell me. No one seemed to think it was a big deal.

Should I not worry about it either? They're the professionals, right?

It wasn't normal for me to be constipated, and it seemed to be getting worse instead of getting better. Upon conveying the doctor's response to my parents, my mom wanted me to come home for testing. Since I only had a few weeks left of school, I convinced her that we could just get it checked out when I got home to Canada for the summer. After all, besides the constipation and bloating, I was feeling totally normal. No reason to freak out, right?

There I go, discrediting my intuition again.

RAISED ON WESTERN MEDICINE

"The reason you have a hard time trusting your intuition
is because you are still convinced that some outside authority
knows better than you."
– Maryam Hasnaa

When I was young, we always went to the doctor when we were sick. It was what everyone did. We treated our bodies like machines that needed a diagnosis and a remedy in order to get back to working order. Being sick meant something was wrong with you, and the doctor was the one who had the power to fix you. When this is the environment that you are immersed in, you learn that doctors know better than you do. You learn to discount your body's natural ability to heal, repair, and restore balance.

Couple this learning with my experience in sports, and you have a recipe for expecting medical experts to fix you. I frequented massage therapists, physiotherapists, and sports therapists for the better part of my high school and university years. My body was probably asking for a break, but the mentality in athletics is if you take a break or miss a game, you are falling behind. There wasn't any time to rest and relax. Progress was about practicing harder to perform better, and that mentality swallowed me up. Looking up to the professionals that helped my body stay in peak working order, I became fascinated by the body and how it worked, which led me to study sports medicine.

My sports medicine classes filled my mind with all kinds of learning and beliefs about the body, health, and recovery. Most of my classes were about how to test, diagnose, and fix the body when it was injured; but we also dove into the workings of the body from anatomy to exercise physiology, nutrition to pharmacology, and beyond. Our focus was only on the physical body, which was all I ever knew and became all I valued. There was no talk about mental health, emotional wellness, or how we are complex, multifaceted beings because that is not how western medicine functions. Instead, it looks at the physical symptoms, breaks up the body into its systems and parts, and attempts to treat them all individually.

Western medicine's miss is that it only focuses on the physical, rather than the interconnectedness of the mental, emotional, spiritual, and physical aspects of self. So, what do you do when you have a feeling, a nudge, or an internal knowing that shows up in your body? And what happens when your body is trying to speak to you, but all you know about health is the physical body?

SPRINGFEST

Spring was a stunning time in Erie. The cherry blossoms were in bloom, the summer sun beamed down, and everyone was antsy to enjoy the warm weather. It was my junior year of college and, like all spring trimesters, it was so much fun. Beach volleyball courts were consumed by students. Basketball courts housed sweaty guys in sleeveless shirts. Picnic tables were occupied with students studying, socializing, or devouring a barbequed meal as the tasty aromas filled the air. Campus was dotted with students who had convinced their professors to allow them to sit outside to absorb their lecture. It was the most wonderful time of the year in Erie, which meant one thing was on the horizon. The biggest weekend of the year on campus was about to arrive: Springfest.

Springfest was a giant weekend party on campus to celebrate the end of the school year. The best way to depict this epic college weekend was to refer to the college parties you see in the movies. Springfest was next level across the board, and it was a guaranteed good time. Every year, the campus grounds were flooded with activities, events, and students galore. The quad hosted all kinds of games, from a human hamster ball to a Velcro wall, sumo suits to the balancing Q-tip battle, and giant boxing gloves. The new attraction this year was the smash-a-car, which was surrounded by spray paint bottles and baseball bats. Students were encouraged to decorate and demolish the old car. Our gymnasium even hosted a concert for bands like Lifehouse and Great Big Sea. It was the only weekend students didn't have to be worried about getting in trouble for drinking on campus. So, you can imagine the shenanigans that ensued.

Friday after class, to kick start the weekend, my friend, Christine, and I went over to our buddy's apartment for a Saskatchewan paralyzer pitcher party. The three of us were from Saskatchewan and had become close friends. Since no one else on campus knew what paralyzers were—a mixed drink of Kahlua, vodka, milk, and pop—we teamed up to create our own fun, while our buddy, Meds, had agreed to make us his famous scrambled eggs with a melted cheese slice on top. We were living the college dream! When we finished our meal and cranked up the fun, we relocated to the living room where some of our guy friends were playing video games. With bandanas tied around their foreheads and light sabre toys in their hands, it was obvious they had been drinking long before we had arrived. Hilarity ensued, like it always did with this crew.

As more people continued to show themselves into the apartment, that was the night that I first laid eyes on my future husband.

"Ohhhhhhhh!" All the guys yelled as a muscular dreamboat graced the apartment and plopped down on the couch.

Holy! Who is that? I wondered.

I casually checked Mr. Muscles out without being obvious about it, as one of his rough-around-the-edges teammates were sure to call me out on it if they caught my eyes wandering.

He had bright blue eyes and dark, curly hockey hair spilling out from under his hat. His bulging musculature was visible through his shirt from every angle. His eyes lit up when he smiled, and he had no problem dishing insults back to the guys when required. Our eyes met and we smiled at each other. My stomach did a flip, and I quickly looked away as my cheeks began to feel flushed. I took a deep breath to keep my cool. The last thing I needed was for one of the guys to call me out on my flushed face.

"Pierce!" I heard a friend call out as a beer was thrown in his direction.

I made a mental note, assuming that was his last name.

The shenanigans continued for the rest of the weekend, but I kept my eye on Mr. Muscles as our paths continued to cross. Each time our eyes met, our smiles continued to grow. I'd catch him looking at me. Then he would catch me looking at him. Eventually, I worked up the nerve to talk to him. And that was where our story began.

Over the final two weeks of class, I found myself constantly wondering when our paths would cross again. Luckily, a small campus, an overlapping circle of friends, and social media worked in our favour and allowed our connection to grow. I felt nervous that whatever spark had been lit between us would fade away over the summer. But as our interest in each other continued to blossom, we exchanged numbers and agreed to stay in touch over the summer—a summer that would stretch and redefine me in ways I could have never seen coming.

LAND OF LIVING SKIES

My teammate and former roommate, Christine, and I were eager to be homeward bound. We packed our lives up into my green Grand Prix and hot tailed it out of the campus parking lot as soon as we handed in our last exam. As we began the thirty-hour journey home to Saskatchewan, my foot fell heavy on the gas pedal. The beautiful summertime weather was stirring our souls and we were both looking forward to being reunited with friends and family.

After dropping Christine off, I headed out of Saskatoon on a highway I knew like the back of my hand. I breathed in the familiarity and smiled, then cranked up the music and took in the view. The music moved my soul and the air conditioning blew through my hair as the warm sun danced on my skin. As familiar sights filled the windshield, a sense of freedom and comfort took hold. Before I knew it, I was pulling into my hometown and turning down the familiar roads of my childhood.

My grandparents were always on the top of my list to visit upon returning home. They moved their life from Saskatoon to Rosetown when my dad was five years old to begin a Goodyear tire dealership, which my dad and uncle then took over as adults. Growing up with my grandparents in the same town was a great experience. When my brothers and I were little, we would often walk to their house after school, stop in for visits, and have sleepovers when my parents were away. Grandma would watch our track and field days in elementary school and, as we grew up, both Grandma and Grandpa would attend my brothers' hockey games and my volleyball games. When high school came along, Grandma needed assistance around the house due to arthritis, so I would clean for her every two weeks and help her wrap presents for Christmas. We grew very close over the years and my grandparents had a special place in my heart.

As I pulled up to the front of their house, Grandma appeared in the doorway, awaiting my grand entrance. "Well isn't this a lovely surprise! I thought you weren't getting home until tomorrow!" she said, bright-eyed and beaming.

"Christine and I got on the road right after our last exam, so we made good time," I said as I made my way up the front steps and gave her a big hug.

"You've lost weight," she said instantly, as she released me from her arms and led me into the house to catch up.

"Oh, not really," I lied, knowing that it was visible, as I plopped down on my usual spot on the couch. I was skinny—we're talking abnormally skinny—besides my slightly protruding abdomen. I had always had a strong, athletic build, so of course it was noticeable when my usual jeans had been replaced with a pair two sizes smaller.

"Your mom said you haven't been feeling good," she queried, letting me know that she was in the loop.

I brushed it off. "Well, it has mostly just been constipation and feeling bloated. She booked me a doctor's appointment for next week, I think."

"Oh, well that's great, darlin'. I hope they get to the bottom of it for you."

"Me too," I agreed.

Grandma always brought a sense of comfort for me. Maybe it was her demeanour, our connection, how I always knew what to expect, or the way her house never changed. Maybe it was the way she always encouraged me, told me she was proud, and appreciated every minute I spent with her.

After catching up, I asked, "Is Grandpa at work?" knowing full well that he was.

"Yes, he is. You'll have to stop over at the tire shop to see him. Are you coming over for lunch tomorrow?" Grandma asked as our visit came to an end.

"You know I'd love to."

"It's a date then. I'll let Grandpa know," she said, proudly.

Grandma's specialty was making her famous macaroni for lunch, so I usually arranged for a lunch time visit to get my fix of her cooking and another visit to warm my heart. While Grandma's macaroni was nothing fancy, it had become a special type of comfort food for my brothers and I. Walking into their house to the aroma of noodles cooking on the stove made me instantly feel at ease. Her macaroni, coupled with bologna, chocolate milk, a plate of store-bought cookies, and a catch-up conversation rounded out the experience I so often longed for when I was thirty hours away from home.

WHISPERS BECOME SCREAMS

"Life is constantly knocking at our door,
trying to push open our windows that we may see more;
and if out of fear we lock the doors, bolt all the windows,
the knocking only grows louder."
– Jiddu Krishnamurti

Mom had booked doctor's appointment for the week after I returned home. She remained adamant about getting to get to the bottom of whatever was going on inside my body. Dr. Dion, was a kind and sweet soul and he had been the our family doctor throughout my high school years. After Mom had initially voiced her concerns to him when booking the appointment, he agreed that I should come in for some testing. However, with my only symptoms being constipation, bloating, and the new ones of frequent urination and mild weight loss, we didn't have many clues to work with. After his examination of my abdomen, he concluded that I was constipated and should eat more fibre.

I mean, really? Again? Right after I just explained what the campus doctors had repeatedly told me? I felt confused. Did the doctors not trust me? Or did they just think nothing of it? My symptoms were mild and fairly commonplace, I'd give them that...but they weren't normal for me. That should have been worthy of further examination.

Even though I had been eating plenty of fibre, he wanted me to try Metamucil first to see if that would help get things moving before proceeding with more testing. Mom was not satisfied with this answer.

Seriously? I questioned. *Another dismissive diagnosis. Something is wrong, people!*

And this is when I first began to realize that doctors are human.

Doctors are not all-knowing deities. They can't see into your body. They do not know everything about the human body, its functions, and all of the possible illnesses and complications, even if we might like and expect them to. They are human, just like the rest of us. They make mistakes. They don't know it all. Doctors do their best from their level of understanding, which is exactly why we cannot give them all the power. Because when we do, we discount our inner knowing and our own healing power.

This part of the story is a big deal because it is when I learned not to give my power away. This is when I began to realize what I now know: The messages from your body are valid, even if the medical experts don't believe you.

So, even when there aren't a lot of conscious, visible, tangible clues, but you know in your heart that something is off, don't give professional opinions merit over your inner knowing. When something feels off, it probably is.

My mom doesn't take shit from anyone. She speaks her mind, she's smart, determined, and sometimes abrasive. She was just as confused as I was, but she knew that whatever was going on was more than just a constipation issue, and she wasn't about to let it slide. She does not settle, give up, or take no for an answer when she has a feeling otherwise. So, upon arriving home from the appointment, Mom not only mixed a glass of Metamucil for me, but mixed one for herself, too. It was time for an experiment.

Later that day, Mom enjoyed the view of the inside of the bathroom as the Metamucil worked its way through her intestines and into the toilet. I, on the other hand, didn't have to go at all.

"Come on!" Mom said in disbelief. "You don't have to go at all? You've got to at least try."

"Seriously? Do you not believe me?" I said, appalled.

"How is it not affecting you at all? You must have to go."

"What do you think I am—a toddler, that you have to tell me to go?" I said with disbelief plastered all over my face. "But, fine. I'll go 'try'," I rolled my eyes. "Just don't hold your breath."

And into the bathroom I went, only to disappoint my mother.

A couple of weeks went by and I began to look more and more frail with each passing day. I was a bag of bones and my stamina was rapidly disintegrating. Climbing a flight of stairs had me winded and gasping for air, which was a major red flag. Hell, only months prior, I was running an exorbitant amount of shuttle sprints at volleyball practice until I was on the verge of vomiting.

What is happening inside of me? I wondered.

Mom was getting more and more concerned. At mealtimes, I could barely eat more than a few bites of food before I felt full. When I ate a couple extra bites to appease my parents instead of listening to my body, then nausea surfaced. My lack of appetite brought with it an onslaught of jabbing remarks from my brothers about being anorexic.

"Oh, screw off!" I snapped. "I literally can't eat any more than this without feeling sick!" I barked at them. Anger coursed through my body. Never had I felt so judged, attacked, and unsupported. I wondered if they felt the daggers I was throwing at them with my eyes. I got up from the table and stormed off to my room.

As my health continued to deteriorate, I came to the end of my rope. I'd been home for almost a month and we still hadn't figured a single thing out. The next morning, Mom brought the bathroom scale up from the basement and set it down on the kitchen floor. "If you weigh less than 140 pounds, we are going back to the doctor right now," she declared.

I stepped on the scale... 142. "YES!" I exclaimed, sarcastically, accompanied by an overly dramatic fist pump and a wide smile.

Shaking her head, she confirmed, "We are going anyway."

With no "relief" from our Metamucil experiment and my symptoms growing worse by the day, we had to get to the bottom of this. My appetite was nonexistent, and my energy levels had plummeted. After filling the doctor in, he ordered blood work and had my come back the next morning for a small bowel follow-through.

That weekend, my symptoms worsened. It felt like I ran out of steam each evening, my temples ached, and my eyes felt as though I'd had a fist full of sand thrown in them at Mach speed. I would cautiously move from the couch to my bed and back again. Soon, my body felt achy all over. After a rough weekend in which I could not have possibly felt any worse, we went back to the doctor for the results of my follow-through test and blood work, desperately hoping for some answers.

"Well, your small bowel follow-through results came back normal," Dr. Dion said as he looked at my chart with a frown. "But, your blood work is unusual... your hemoglobin is low, and your creatinine is high, which means that your kidney function must be impaired." After filling him in on the progression of my symptoms, he called the hospital to request an urgent ultrasound.

The next morning, I was squeezed in for an abdominal ultrasound. We raced up to the hospital at 8:00 a.m. in the morning. for blood work and then were directed to the waiting room for an ultrasound at 8:40 a.m. As my nerves skyrocketed, Schar, the mom of my high school best friend, Brittany, poked her head into the waiting room, then came over when she saw us. As she talked with mom, I remembered how often I admired her and her daughter for embodying such rock-solid confidence. It was then that she put her hands on my shoulders and looked me in the eyes with a fiery determination I'd seen time and time again. "Whatever happens, you're going to be okay," she said. "Do you hear me? I mean it."

I nodded as I blinked back the tears that had begun to pool in my eyes.

"I'm serious. You've got this," she repeated without a shadow of a doubt as she dipped her chin and raised her eyebrow. "You know I wouldn't say it if it wasn't true."

My throat tightened, knowing I believed her. All I could do was nod and force a teary smile.

She hugged me so tight, I could feel it in my soul. Then she kissed me on the cheek and was off.

As I sat in the waiting room chair, trying not to bawl my eyes out, my name was called. I stood and followed a technician through the hallways of the hospital to a stale, sanitized exam room. As I climbed onto the exam table, the crinkling noise of the paper echoed through the silence of the room. I laid on the exam table in the awkward silence and looked down at my scrawny body and protruding tummy.

The ultrasound tech explored my abdomen like it was a mysterious deep-sea dive into the unknown. Somewhere inside, a feeling took hold, screaming that the results of this ultrasound wouldn't be good, but the technician didn't show a trace of concern on her face. I knew she wasn't allowed to tell me anything, but I couldn't help but wonder what she was discovering inside my abdomen.

SPITFIRE PEP TALK

"She was a wild one;
always stomping on eggshells that everyone else tiptoed on."
– Kaitlin Foster

As the tech was performing the abdominal exam, my mind drifted to a memory of a grade eight basketball game, and all of a sudden, I was there. I could hear the shoes squeaking on the gym floor, the bouncing of the basketball, the referee's whistle, and the sound of my teammates calling out to one another. The smell of half-time oranges wafted into my nostrils as I looked over to the bleachers to see my parents and grandparents sitting in the front row.

I was paired up with an opponent who towered over me and had an extra thirty pounds on me. She was like a brick wall with elbows, and I struggled to hold my ground against her. She kept pushing me around, and I kept letting her. When coach called a time out, I noticed my best friend's mom, the same one from the hospital, motion for me to come over to her at the end of the court. Confused, I ran over. Little did I know, I was about to get a pep talk that would shape my life moving forward.

"Don't you let that girl push you around just because she's bigger than you. You stand your ground. Now, go get in there and keep your elbows up. Got it?" she said with a look of wild determination plastered all over her face as she stared through my eyes and directly into my soul.

I nodded. She smiled with a fiery look in her eyes that I recognized from her daughter. "You get in there and be aggressive. Go show us how it's done."

At that moment I could see exactly where my best friend got her spunk from. She was a spitfire just like her mom. And her mom saw that spunk within me, too, just waiting to be lit up.

Sure, there had been moments when I put my guard down and channelled my inner spitfire, but it had never become the norm for me. I was too used to playing by the rules and being respectful, which didn't always translate into feisty, athletic prowess.

As I ran back towards my team, stunned, something changed inside me. I went back out on that court and played like I had never played before.

Getting a pep talk from someone I looked up to was exactly what I needed to give myself permission to stand my ground, play to my potential, quit being afraid of messing up, and stop taking shit from anyone—on or off the court.

Little did I know that this memory was the exact reminder I needed while I laid on the ultrasound table. Now was not the time to get tossed around by the tide. It was time to channel my courage and my inner spitfire.

THE PHONE CALL

The doctor's office called within hours of my ultrasound. Mom answered the phone, and I watched her intently, trying to decipher her facial expression.

The thought, "This can't be good," echoed through my mind.

"They asked us to come down to the clinic right away," Mom said as she hung up the phone. We looked at each other with blank expressions, unsure of how to react. We were both scared, but neither my mom nor I knew what to say to each other, so we faked positivity all the while knowing that what we were about to find out might be devastating.

While Mom called Dad at work to tell him to meet us at the doctor's office, I needed to talk to someone, too. As panic washed over me, I found myself dialling Mark's number. In our short conversation, I heard myself say out loud, "I probably have cancer."

"Don't say that," he retorted.

"Well, I probably do."

Was I trying to prepare myself for the blow that was about to sucker punch me in the gut? Or did I intuitively know what was at war inside my body? Maybe it was both.

Mom and I sat in the doctor's office in silence, listening to the creaks of the floorboards as footsteps moved passed our room. I felt wildly nervous as I sat on the exam table. The paper crinkling underneath me with my every move. My stomach curled in knots as we waited for the verdict to be delivered. Terror slithered up my spine, and I felt chilled as my back muscles tightened and my hands turned to ice. I continually blinked back tears as I put on a brave face and shoved my emotions back down where I thought they belonged—out of sight.

Finally, the doorknob turned, and everything began to move in slow motion. As Dr. Dion entered the room, I took a deep breath, hoping I had made up a much bigger story in my mind than the reality he was about to deliver. As his eyes grew teary, it hit me.

This is really, really bad.

After I heard the words tumour and cancer, all the other words faded away. It felt as though I had been smacked in the back of the head by a massive wave and was pulled under by the undertow. My jaw tightened and emotions flooded my body as I vigorously tried to blink back the tears that were rapidly filling my eyes. Mom instantly hugged me and cried. Dr. Dion supported us with overflowing empathy as he wiped his tear-stained cheeks.

Then, the sound of the doorknob grabbed our attention. We all turned to see the nurse letting my dad into the room. As my eyes met with Dad's, the flood gates opened and I turned into a puddle.

After a few minutes of tears and desperation, Mom snapped into her best survival mode: taking action. "Where do we go from here?" she asked, as she tried to regain her composure.

"Start by going home to pack your bags, then head up to the hospital in town. They know you're coming, so your room will be ready. You will get transferred to the Royal University Hospital in Saskatoon tomorrow. There, you'll be put through a lot of tests to discover what exactly this tumour is."

I was in shock. *How can this be?* I wondered. But in the next moment, I could hear a voice whisper in my mind, "I was right."

Mom and I climbed into her SUV and Dad into his truck, and we attempted to pull ourselves together, driving home in silence.

While my mind raced, I could not bring myself to form an audible sentence. Waves of tears surfaced from behind my eyes like an emotional tide slamming into the shore. My chest felt like it carried the weight of a thousand elephants, making a deep breath almost too much to bear. My body shivered in fear right through the summer heat. This is how drowning feels, I realized, as I gasped for air.

When we got home, Mom and Dad exchanged some words, periodically sniffled, wiped their eyes, and tried to put on brave faces for me. I could sense the fear circulating among us—it was palpable.

"It's going to be okay," they tried to convince themselves and me.

I nodded, still reeling.

What do you pack to take to the hospital at a time like this?

I robotically moved around my bedroom collecting necessary items then stuffed them into a duffle bag. Comfortable clothes, check. Toothbrush, check. Music and earphones, check. Pillow, check. I attempted to focus my mind on packing, but the diagnosis consumed my mind. I found a few more items I hoped would distract me or provide comfort.

"Ready?" Mom asked.

"I think so," I lied as the oxygen was continually ripped from my lungs. I held my pillow in front of my torso like a shield, wishing it was all just a bad dream.

How can I ever be ready for this? I frowned.

As we opened the door to the garage, my brother, Kiel, was returning home from work. While he normally lived in Saskatoon with our brother, he had moved home for the summer to work at my dad's tire shop, while Kenton remained in Saskatoon for an engineering summer job. The typical tire shop scent of rubber consumed Kiel and smacked me in the nose.

"What's up?" he asked, all chipper. "Where are you guys going?"

His questions were too much for me to handle. Every ounce of energy I had was being used to hold myself together. As I briefly looked at him, my throat closed, and all words disappeared. Panicked, I moved past him, climbed down the stairs and got back into the car. Mom's eyes grew teary as she followed closely behind me.

"Are you going to be back soon?" he asked, visibly confused.

We forced faked smiles, unable to form a shred of optimism, and proceeded to report to our small-town hospital; leaving him, unanswered, and standing in the garage.

My brother entered the house, taken aback by our strange reaction. He knew something was off. As he repeated his question to Dad, "Where are Kristin and Mom going?" Dad broke down into tears. He no longer had to put on a brave face for us. He hugged Kiel and sobbed uncontrollably, barely able to form any words.

Dad was our protector. He got fierce when he had to, laid down the law when he was determined he knew what was best for us, and would never let anyone mess with his family. Inside, he had the heart of a teddy bear. On the outside, he had an intimidating exterior that had often scared off my guy friends from raising any hell under our roof. To us, Dad always lent a listening ear, provided feedback, and became a sounding board for many of our major life decisions. He was a sturdy support system that we could always lean on.

Seeing Dad in this state struck Kiel in the chest. Kiel's confusion grew, but he knew whatever was going on was not good at all. He had barely ever seen Dad cry before, let alone break down into tears. As he stood there poised, he comforted Dad as he finally heard the words squeak from Dad's mouth, "Kristin has cancer."

HOMETOWN HOSPITAL HOPE

"The moment you change your perception
is the moment you rewrite the chemistry of your body."
– Bruce Lipton

Upon our arrival to my hometown hospital, we were shown to the room where I would spend the night before being transported to Saskatoon. In small-town Saskatchewan, you know everyone, or at least your parents do, and this was no exception. The nurse, Evelyn, came in wearing white scrubs and a white nursing hat, the really old school type. She greeted my mom by her first name, then took my vitals.

Although the nurse knew me, she didn't look at me with sorrow or pity, which I was both surprised about and thankful for. I had no idea what to think or how I felt about the news because it had all happened so fast. I felt as though my heart and voice box had been ripped out and stomped on. I struggled to inhale breath into my tight lungs. An endless stream of questions and thoughts flew through my mind at lightning speed.

What is happening right now? Is this a sick dream?! I'm twenty-one years old!

Besides the fact that my mind was racing with questions, I didn't even know what to say. I felt steamrolled by the news, unable to formulate a sentence. Thankfully, my mom did all the talking. In the midst of her questions, her voice got shaky, and then she got quiet. I looked over to see tears streaming down her cheeks.

When I saw Mom crying about this fairly large mountain of a problem in front of me, it completely set me off. The nurse went over to hug Mom. Before I even knew it, I lost my cool. "If you're going to cry, you need to do it in the hallway!" I snapped, which probably came out snippier than I had intended it to.

WHOA. Where the heck did that come from? I was so triggered by her tears. But, why?

Mom's emotions triggered me because, to me, tears meant weakness, which I boiled down to defeat. Her tears brought my fear to the surface from the depths of where I was desperately trying to keep it at bay. Anger was just my surface emotion, but there's always something beneath the surface of anger.

I was confused, overwhelmed, and full of my own emotions that I had no idea what to do with hers. All I knew was that I was incredibly scared and overloaded, and I thought that everyone's tears and fears about this terrifying news would not help me get through my own. The mirror of fear pushed me over my emotional edge. It was not the time for me to be weak and vulnerable. It didn't feel safe to be either. I didn't feel safe to allow my emotions to show because, to me, that meant I was admitting weakness and defeat. And that was not how we were going to kick off this uphill journey into the unknown.

Subconsciously, I must have I felt as though I needed to set the stage for the difficult challenge ahead. While we didn't know what was happening inside my body, I did what I knew best and a decision was made: We weren't going to cry and whine over this. I would not feel sorry for myself or mope around. I would muster up every ounce of courage and face this head-on. I was twenty-one and this wasn't the end. It wasn't even close to the end.

I realize, in hindsight, that stuffing my emotions and maintaining a façade of composure was a huge part of what got me into the cancer mess in the first place. There could have been a much better way to handle my mom expressing her emotions. She didn't deserve that. But I was doing the best I could in the midst of a terrifying situation, even if it didn't seem like it. As Maya Angelou said, "When you know better, you do better."

"Have you heard about BodyTalk?" the nurse interjected, likely in an attempt to break the tension.

"No, we haven't," Mom said. "What is that?"

"I don't know what it is, but I just felt like I needed to tell you. There is a girl from Biggar (Saskatchewan) who does it. It might be worth giving her a call."

Just like that—a nurse who had an intuitive hunch and trusted it enough to tell us had delivered our godsend. At the exact moment, when we felt so helpless and hopeless, confused and uncertain, devastated and defeated, and overwhelmed and speechless, this nurse had offered us hope. In that outdated hospital room, the nurse, intuitively, gave me permission to hold some of my healing power in my own hands. She gave us permission to not hand over my fate to the doctors—regardless of the more detailed news that would soon come our way.

In that moment, my mom and I grabbed that rope of hope and pulled ourselves from bobbing helplessly in an ocean of despair.

It was not the end. It couldn't be.

WHATEVER IT TAKES

"Something had to give. It wasn't going to be my life."
– Kristin Pierce

In a recent podcast interview, I was asked about my experience with cancer and my introduction to BodyTalk. Upon sharing the story of the nurse who recommended BodyTalk, the interviewer asked how open I was to holistic therapies when I found out I had cancer. In all honesty, I wasn't. I hadn't even considered holistic therapies to be an actual thing before this timely introduction. My studies focused on the physical body, and in being so left-brained, that was all I knew.

But, when you're standing in the presence of a devastating health crisis, you're either willing to open your mind and do whatever it takes or you're not.

Within four days of initially hearing about BodyTalk, I received my first session, followed by four more sessions in that first week, and weekly sessions thereafter for the duration of my treatment. This was my "TSN turning point". I was willing to open my minds to anything that might help. I was willing to do whatever it took because I had nothing to lose.

In the realm of holistic health, it is not uncommon to hear stories of devastating health crises, accidents, or loss of loved ones that led people to their introduction to BodyTalk or other holistic modalities. It is not uncommon for people to hit rock bottom before they are willing to open their minds, take a good look in the mirror, and search for a new way. And, that is okay. Sometimes you need to be stuck between a rock and a hard place before you're ready for change. Better late than never.

BodyTalk blew my mind along with the incredible wisdom that surfaced because of it. Emotionally and mentally, I began the process (with a whole lot of assistance) of reassessing my definition of health by moving inside myself to reveal and release all that I had been holding onto and stuffing down. Like all healing, it was definitely a process, but BodyTalk was the key that taught me how to understand, connect with, and support myself, while being supported through the most devastating experience of my life.

I believe that being willing to open your mind was instrumental in my healing. Opening my mind to BodyTalk, coupled with a "whatever it takes" determination carried me through.

Cancer would not be the end of my story. It would, instead, become the greatest catalyst of change in my entire life.

TWENTY WEEKS

*"Don't let the noise of others' opinions
drown out your own inner voice."*
– Steve Jobs

When we arrived at Royal University Hospital in Saskatoon, I was placed in an awkward emergency room cubicle for what felt like an eternity. The room was bordered by curtains and we could hear every not-so-private conversation happening around us in every direction.

When the doctors arrived to conduct an initial exam, I was asked if a student doctor could participate on my exam. I agreed without a moment's hesitation, since I had been given the same grace when shadowing physiotherapists and surgeries time and time again. Of course I would let a student be involved.

When performing my pelvic and abdominal exam, it became a fairly regular occurrence for doctors to comment on how strong and muscular my abdomen was.

Every physician who touched my abdomen said, "Wow, you are very muscular."

Really? I thought, taken aback. Since I'd always been an athlete, my "normal" didn't seem that impressive to me.

Continuing my exam, the doctor stated to the resident, "Now, if she was pregnant—and we know you aren't," he reassured me, "How far along would she be by how much her abdomen is showing?"

The resident got out his tape measure and placed it on my belly, measuring from my pubic bone to the top of my growing abdominal bump. "Twenty weeks," he declared.

"Yes, that is right," the doctor confirmed.

Halfway to a full-term baby?! My stomach is protruding that much?! My medical mind was fascinated until I was brought back to the reality that I was the patient this time, rather than the observer. I needed some time to let that sink in.

Whatever was growing in my abdomen was large and cancerous. However, no one could determine what type of tumour it was, which organs were affected, or if it had spread.

"We get some bloodwork drawn here shortly and will try to get you in for a CT scan tonight to see if we can get a better picture of what's going on here," the doctor noted.

At 11:00 p.m., we were still in that same lovely curtained cubicle in the ER, unintentionally eavesdropping on every conversation within a twenty-foot radius. After what felt like an eternity, a doctor finally appeared to say I was booked for a CT scan and that hopefully they would have a bed open for me by the time the test ended. After my blood work results came back, the doctor advised that I would not be able to have a typical CT scan procedure because it wasn't safe to give me the dye due to impaired kidney function. However, I still needed the CT scan for the doctors to get a picture of which what was happening inside my abdomen, so they decided to proceed with the CT scan without the use of dye.

Finally, a wheelchair and chauffeur arrived to get me out of the emergency room hell hole that I'd been stuck in for twelve whole noisy, uncomfortable hours. *Hallelujah!* I thought. *Get me out of here!* Little did I know what was coming next.

With my parents following closely behind, I was wheeled through a maze of corridors that would eventually connect to an elevator. The long, winding hallways were dimly lit and gave off an eerie kind of feeling. As the tired wheelchair driver pushed my weary body in awkward silence, it seemed as though we were weaving through the deepest crevices of the intestines of the hospital.

After exiting the elevator, we were delivered to the CT waiting room for more... waiting. Have you ever noticed how uncomfortable the chairs are in hospital waiting rooms? The hard, plastic chairs didn't ease my fatigue or apprehension. Realistically, it wasn't the chairs that were uncomfortable, it was me. And the chairs wouldn't let me hide it. By now, I was too tired to smile or care about who else was waiting for a scan.

Eventually, a technician emerged with a chart in hand. "Kristin Peterson?"

"Yes, that's me," I replied. After the initial conversation and questions, it didn't take long for me to realize these technicians were not happy campers. Are they tired, too? I wondered.

Then came the onslaught of doubtful looks and visible disbelief in my responses.

"Can you confirm when your last period was?"

"Yes, around May 20th," I said.

"Can you confirm that you aren't pregnant?"

"Yes," I replied, feeling somewhat embarrassed that they were asking me these questions in front of my parents and a waiting room of strangers. Of course, they had to ask, but I had already answered all of these questions in the ER.

"How sure are you that you aren't pregnant?" the technician asked.

"Umm..." I said, confused, "I'm pretty sure," I noted, somewhat sarcastically. *Is this seriously happening?* I wondered, as I shot an unimpressed look at my parents.

I could tell the technicians were not impressed with me or my answers. I didn't know I would be under interrogation in front of the entire waiting room before my scan. It felt like everyone was staring at me, and all I wanted to do was crawl into a hole. I could feel the blood flushing my cheeks. Instead, I took a breath and said, "My symptoms started mildly in the end of February, but I kept getting my period as usual."

"Ok, so are you one hundred percent sure?"

Good lord! Well, I was until now! Prior to my cancer diagnosis, being pregnant had never even crossed my mind. What does a medical emergency have to do with being pregnant at all? I later found out that you can't have a CT scan if you're pregnant because the radiation can harm the baby.

I'm not pregnant, right? I panicked.

"I'm sure!" I said, exasperated. I shot a look of desperation at Mom and Dad.

I understood the technicians were doing their job, but I could tell they truly didn't believe me and were making it blatantly obvious, which I didn't appreciate. Their intense doubt and grilling session made me start to question what I knew to be true for myself.

NO. I am not pregnant. Or, shit, am I? I think that's when I got my last period. Or did I dream that up?

I began to question everything I had known to be true for myself and my body. I'd never felt so overcome by doubt and fear in my life. My mind raced. *Please don't let it be a baby. Please don't let it be a baby.*

As I went in for the CT scan, the technicians' facial expressions, mannerisms, glances, and actions were extremely cold and had me feeling like they were blatantly send me the message that they were unimpressed. I climbed up on the scanning table and obeyed their instructions. The table felt hard and cold. As the machine moved me into the CT scanner, the technician began to deliver instructions through a speaker: Inhale, hold...release. Exhale all the way, hold...and breathe.

As I obediently listened to their commands, I couldn't help but hear the voice screaming inside my head, "Please don't be pregnant. Please don't be pregnant. Dear God, please don't let me be pregnant."

When the scan ended, their expressions softened. Technicians are not allowed to tell you results, but I knew from the subtle softening of their expressions that I was definitely not pregnant. I wanted to throw up my middle finger at them, but I politely refrained.

As I walked out of the scanning room, relief washed over my body the moment I locked eyes with my parents. With deep breaths, I attempted to calm my nerves as I was wheeled up to a hospital room by a new wheelchair chauffeur.

Embarrassing and traumatizing—that's what that was.

LET'S TALK ABOUT SEX

L et's talk about sex—actually, let's not. Open discussions about sexuality still bring up feelings of discomfort for me. Sex was not a topic that was openly discussed in our family. Besides the basic "birds and the bees" conversation, I never talked to my parents about hardly anything relating to sexuality, boyfriends, or even periods for that matter. We skirted, side-stepped, and mostly avoided these conversations at all costs—well, I did anyways. Avoidance was a major coping mechanism. So, imagine the excruciating discomfort and embarrassment I felt being bombarded with questions about my sexual health, reproductive organs, and menstrual cycle, in front of my parents and numerous doctors.

When I got my period for the first time, I was at the lake with my friend and her family. I told my friend and she graciously coached me through the situation. But upon returning home, I didn't tell my mom. A week later, with tears pouring down her cheeks, she asked me why I hadn't told her. I was confused by her tears. I barely allowed my thoughts or emotions outside of myself, so why was she expecting me to open up for this? Why in the world would I want to share that news with anyone? To me, the changes happening within my body were weird and out of my control. I was not about to shout it from the rooftops.

A PLETHORA OF TESTS

"When we have no words to speak. The body does it for us."
– Unknown

I spent the next day in a hospital room where I was poked, prodded, and palpated by so many doctors I couldn't keep count. My hospital room was a revolving door of different doctors and experts asking to examine me. I seemed to be a peculiar case, which had them interested, intrigued, and eager to discover what was wrong with me, as if the winning diagnosis would deliver noble bragging rights. I couldn't help but feel like a medical freak show that they all wanted to be a part of. Then, they huddled in the hallway to talk about me, and ordered test after test: blood work, urinalysis, external ultrasound, x-rays, internal ultrasound, and more blood work.

This was another defining moment. These highly trained doctors were baffled. While I was understanding towards the doctors, my dad was fuming with anger and questioning their authority. They were throwing darts in the dark and it began to open my eyes even more to the fact that, as a society, we put doctors on a pedestal. It didn't mean they weren't doing their best. It also didn't mean that their findings wouldn't have any validity. It simply meant that we shouldn't put all our eggs (and healing potential) in their basket.

After lots of confusion, tests, and exams, the doctors explained that the mass in my abdomen was so large it was squishing my stomach, which was suppressing my appetite, and taking up a lot of the space that my intestines would normally use to digest food. This explained the extreme constipation that I had been experiencing—there was no space in my abdomen for anything to get through. They had yet to determine which organ was actually being affected, so onward with diagnostic testing.

"Are you having any kidney pain?" one doctor inquired.

"Umm, no. I don't think so," I replied. "What would that feel like?"

"It's a dull, achy sensation typically felt in your back around here," he said as he placed his palms on his lower back between his ribs and his hips.

"No, I'm not feeling anything there. Why?"

"Well, your tumour is so big it is pinching off your ureters; the tubes that connect your kidneys to your bladder. Those tubes allow your body to get rid of waste through your urine. Because those tubes are being pinched off, your kidneys are not able to drain and are getting toxic. We will need to do a surgical procedure to put stents in your ureters to hold them open so the kidneys can drain."

When I woke up the next morning, I felt a dull, achy sensation in my back radiating through to my abdomen. Ouch.

Did the kidney pain show up because it was implied that I should expect it? That very well could have been part of it. However, I was also suppressing a lot of fear that I didn't want anyone to see. When pain arises in the kidneys, it typically resonates with the emotion, fear. It made complete sense that my kidneys were "backed up". I was terrified.

When it comes to body consciousness—which comprises the metaphorical details of the body parts and their associated physical, mental, and emotional roles within the body—the kidneys are about filtering. They typically store the fear we harbour within the body when it is too big to process. It was no wonder that my kidneys had grown toxic. I was overloaded with fear. Those feelings had grown so much in the past few weeks, because I intuitively knew that whatever was happening inside my body was definitely not good. Being the one in the hospital bed and being repeatedly grilled about my experience had cranked up the level of fear.

My body was doing its job of reflecting that awareness for me.

DEMEROL FIRE

"Allow the fires of transformation to burn away
all that doesn't serve you."
– Heather Ash Amara

The pain in my kidneys was on the rise, becoming achy and uncomfortable. I was scheduled for stent surgery the next day, which would provide relief, but first, I needed to sleep to allow my body to prepare for my surgery. After a discussion with Dad, I pushed my call button to sheepishly request some relief for my growing discomfort. In walked a nurse who was clearly not in a good mood and wore a scowl on her face. She barely spoke a word to me and when she did, her tone was abrupt and rude. "What's her problem?" I wondered.

After approval, she returned with a syringe of Demerol. As my dad sat beside me, the nurse hooked up the syringe to my IV then slammed the syringe shut, which pushed the entire dose of Demerol into my arm. My eyes slammed shut, my mouth burst open, and I writhed in agony as I let out a pain-filled shriek that I could not contain no matter how hard I tried.

"AHHHHHHHHH!" I screamed and clutched the bed rail as the fire travelled up my arm and into my chest. The breath was pulled from my lungs, and tears instantaneously flooded out of my eyes. It felt like my vein was literally burning from the inside as the medication climbed up my arm, then travelled into the center of my chest and circulated throughout my body.

When the pain finally dissipated, I gasped and tried to catch my breath.

WHAT THE HELL JUST HAPPENED?!

I looked at the nurse with confusion and desperate for an answer. Instead, she simply unhooked the syringe, picked up the trash, and chucked it in the garbage can without saying a word as she left the room.

Seriously?!

I looked at Dad with wide eyes and tear-soaked cheeks. "Oh my God," I gasped. "What the hell was *that*?!"

"I don't know, but she won't be doing that again," he said. Dad was on fire too. I was his little girl—his Toad (that was his nickname for me)—and he would do anything his power to protect me. He got up and headed to the nursing station to "give that nurse a piece of his mind."

As anger slithered up my spine, I felt like I had been abused. That was not okay. Now, I assumed healthcare practitioners didn't feel called to the profession to induce pain to those already suffering. However, it felt very malicious and she didn't show an ounce of apathy on her face afterwards.

When we spoke to another nurse about the situation, she was surprised that the Demerol injection caused me extreme pain since it normally shouldn't. So in an effort to help minimize the burning pain, she and subsequent nurses tried their best to alternate the Demerol syringe with a saline flush, until the medication weaved its way into my bloodstream. As much as I loathed the kidney pain, I also dreaded the burning that came with the Demerol, right before the relief it provided finally arrived.

Being immersed in athletics taught me a lot about pain and how to push through it. From a mental standpoint, I learned not to succumb to the limiting self-talk that often surfaces when pushing your body to extremes. However, this mentality also forged an understanding that if you give into your symptoms, you'll get left behind. It was much better to just "suck it up." No wonder I had overuse injuries. No wonder I played through the pain instead of listening to my body and risking looking like a wimp. In reality, I was doing more damage to my body, mind, and emotional state by embodying the "no pain, no gain" mentality.

But no matter how much I tried to uphold the façade of strength and mental toughness, my body had finally found a way to force me to listen to it. I was finally at a precipice where I could no longer "play through the pain". It was time to learn how to stop and listen to my body, how to ask for help, and how to receive the support I so dearly needed.

THIS DOESN'T MAKE SENSE

"The search for truth is more powerful than its possession."
– Albert Einstein

I finally cracked that night after the Demerol fire. I couldn't sleep a wink as the floodgates opened and the fear roared through me with a vengeance. It was the first time I really let myself feel the insurmountable fear of my diagnosis. The fear had grown so big. Questions rolled through my head like an endless stream of dialogue as I attempted to make sense of my new reality. *How could this happen? What did I do to deserve this? Why? Why me? How? I'm healthy—how do I get cancer? I don't understand. This doesn't make sense.*

My medical brain then rolled through the possible causes for something to blame. *Diet? Is it the occasional chips and chocolate I always feel so guilty about eating? Grandma had brain cancer—I wonder if it had anything to do with that? Is it from any medication I've been on? What about that one I took for acne? Is it because I use tampons? Should I have used pads instead? Is it because of I had sex before marriage?*

If I had something to blame, then at least there would be a logical reason for all of this, right? Then it would all make sense. If I had something to blame for getting cancer, it meant I could pass the buck of responsibility. I know that would have been a big cop-out and a huge opportunity missed because I never would have had to self-reflect on my participation in my experience, which was exactly why there was no logical explanation waiting for me. The cosmic hammer of cancer was supposed to shake me up so I could wake up to a whole new perspective.

Not having a logical explanation in my mind for my diagnosis allowed me the space to find the answers within myself and embark on a healing journey to make sense of it on my own. And that is exactly how it needed to go.

In moments of pain lies the wonderful gift of self-reflection. And that is the silver lining. Sometimes, this opportunity shows up when you're in the middle of the pain. Other times, you can only reflect and look for the silver lining once you've safely made it through the fire of transformation. At all times, it is healing, helpful, and wildly transformative to lean into those scars and look for the gifts.

STENT SURGERY

While we awaited the return of the head oncologist that would lead my tumour resection surgery, my kidneys were growing toxic. The aching sensation had begun to spread throughout my lower back, so the doctors informed us that a stent surgery was necessary, and soon. They explained that stents are little tubes that would be inserted into my ureters to hold them open so my kidneys could drain properly.

The morning of the stent surgery, we were told that I would be squeezed into a last minute opening in the OR's schedule. Without knowing if I'd have to wait all day, I decided to have a bath to pass the time. As usual, I was left in limbo, waiting to find out the time of my surgery. Within a few minutes of climbing in the tub, the nurse came to give me a thirty-minute warning. The wheelchair chauffeur was on his way up to take me to the operating room. Hearing this, I quickly climbed out of the tub and wrapped myself in a towel. It was time to get the show on the road! Just then, the walls began to spin, so I quickly opened the bathroom door. I could see Mom and the nurse looking at me with concern, right before my vision went fuzzy. I reached for a nearby chair as the nurse reached out for me and helped me sit.

"Are you okay?" Mom asked me.

"I think she was about to faint," the nurse said. "Did you see how pale she turned?"

It took me a moment to get my bearings.

"Sometimes that happens with low blood pressure like she's been experiencing. Please be sure not to stand up too quickly, okay?" the nurse said, "Especially after a bath."

I nodded. *That could have ended badly.*

The nurse handed me a surgical gown to change into before the wheelchair chauffeur arrived to escort me in a wheeled chariot to the operating room. Of course, once I stopped waiting for news, the surgical plans progressed with organized speed. The wheelchair paused in the operating waiting room for a brief moment, before delivering me immediately into the OR. As I climbed onto the surgical table, the doctors stood by in their surgical attire, not one of whom I'd recognized. I watched as the anesthesiologist stood beside the table completing her preparations.

"Have you ever had a spinal before?" the anesthesiologist asked.

Instantly, the anatomy nerd in me got excited. "No, I haven't," I replied, "but I'm a sports medicine student, so I'm excited to find out what it's like!"

"Alright, well I'm sure you'll do great. I'll just explain the procedure to you before we begin so you know what to expect," she said, then began to talk me through the process. "Please put your hands on your opposite shoulders, as if you are hugging yourself, and then lean forward. I will clean your back, then ask you to exhale fully and hold very still while I get the needle in. A lot of patients say it feels like a strong pinch. It will make your legs sleepy right away, then you will also get some sleepy gas to help you stay relaxed throughout the surgery."

I felt the cold sensation of a sterilization wipe on my back, which sent a shiver up my spine. I'd heard that spinal needles weren't the loveliest thing to have shoved into your back, so I attempted to calm myself with my breath while the needle was being prepped. By that point, I had formed the habit of biting my bottom lip whenever I was expecting something to hurt.

"Okay, exhale fully and hold still," the anesthesiologist said. I followed her instructions, and I held my breath until it was over. Surprisingly, the giant needle only felt like a pinch. The anesthesiologist then asked me to move my legs onto the surgical table, noting that I would have to pick them up to move them, as she assisted me from behind. Instantly, my legs were completely useless. I couldn't believe how fast it took effect!

Have you ever woken up with your arm asleep after laying on it funny? Or have you ever sat on your foot for too long? If you have, then you'll know what I'm talking about, to some extent. My legs were fully asleep and completely dead weight. My medical mind thought it was "crazy cool."

I remained awake for my surgery, and had a white sheet hung up from my waist down, leaving me with no awareness of what was happening beneath my waist. The happy gas, alongside the spinal needle, had distorted my sense of time—what was actually longer points of time, felt like mere minutes to me. At one point, I groggily turned my head toward the anesthesiologist and said, "Have they started my surgery yet?"

"They're about halfway done," she replied.

"What?! Really?" I said, surprised. It felt as though I had just laid down on the table.

A little while later, while still in surgery and still feeling the effects of my happy haze, I tried to wiggle my toes and realized that I could move the toes on my right foot. I looked toward the anesthesiologist, probably with a drunken smile, and proudly proclaimed, "I can wiggle my toes."

"No you can't," she replied doubtfully, probably thinking the laughing gas was playing with my mind.

"No, I swear," I replied, "Look." As I wiggled my toes, her eyes grew wide.

"Are you feeling any pain?" she asked quickly, full of concern.

"Nope, nothing. But I can wiggle my toes!" I was proud as a peach. A happy, anesthetized peach. Needless to say, the anesthesiologist then upped my dose and I woke up in the recovery room

THE BODY TALKS

"When you can't put your feelings into words, when it's not safe to express your truth, your deepest pains, your old hurts...sometimes the body does the job for us. Trying to communicate, trying to find a way to clue us in on what we're feeling and what's going on. Listen to the body. Instead of thinking something is "wrong" with it, ask yourself, "What is it trying to tell me?""
– Nick Ortner

The day after my stent surgery, and only four days from when I was first introduced to the idea of it, I had my first BodyTalk session. I had no idea what was in store. Luckily, lying in a hospital bed with a cancerous mass in your abdomen creates a sense of desperation that opens your mind to trying just about anything. Considering I was left-brained, this desperation provided a necessary catalyst to entering this experience with an open mind, rather than the analytical viewpoint I would normally take.

Left-brained tendencies ran in our family. It was what we were taught to value—intelligence, book smarts, common sense, linear reasoning, numbers, math, science—and we excelled at it. Is that because we were expected to? I'm not sure. Regardless, being extremely left-brained doesn't often equate to open-mindedness. It just doesn't. Being over-logical often leads to skepticism. However, magically, on the same day I had my first BodyTalk session, my parents each had a session of their own too.

This was mind-boggling. I love my dad to bits, but at that point, there was no way he would have been open to holistic therapies if his daughter was not lying in a hospital bed. Logic always trumped emotions for him. He could reel any situation in and turn it into a logical black and white answer, teaching us to do the same. Mom, while being more emotional, also had a strong logical mind and could line up any random ducks in a row with an efficiency and ease to be admired for. Luckily, desperation creates a willingness to find a new way. And thank goodness for that. This experience was happening for all of us and with divine timing to shake things up.

The BodyTalk Practitioner, Christina, came to the hospital to do my session. As she arrived, my parents left the room to give us some privacy. I had no idea what to expect, but desperate times call for desperate measures.

"How are you?" she said so kindly, her tone full of empathy and understanding. As these words rolled off her tongue, it felt as though she was already looking directly into my soul.

Whoa, I thought, being taken aback by her warmth and kindness. Instantly, I had a feeling that she was going to be able to see through the protective walls I had built up around my heart. I tried to consciously let my guard down.

Be open, I reminded myself.

As she asked questions, I replied by reciting the facts that I had been regularly regurgitating for the doctors.

"I heard you had stent surgery yesterday?" she asked.

"Yes, I did. It went pretty well. I do have some blood in my urine at the moment. Sorry if that's too much information. I'm basically peeing bright red, and it stings a bit," I said sheepishly. "Otherwise, I'm mostly tired, bloated, constipated, and not very hungry. After all my tests, the doctors still don't know what organ is actually affected by cancer."

"Okay, thank you for sharing that. Have you heard about BodyTalk before?" she inquired.

"A little bit, but I don't really know what it's about or how it works."

She began by explaining how BodyTalk worked. "BodyTalk addresses the whole bodymind and works to re-establish healthy communication within the body. The bodymind is a holistic term for the whole self and the interconnectedness of body and mind. When we experience stress, the lines of communication within the bodymind get disconnected. This distorts how well the body can work together to heal, which can then lead to symptoms and disease."

"Okay, that makes sense," I replied, nodding.

"Our body is always talking to us through symptoms, sensations, and pain. These symptoms usually start out as whispers. However, when we don't listen or pay attention to the messages from our bodies, or we ignore and disregard them, those whispers can get louder and will eventually turn into screams."

I liked how she broke it all down for me. The wheels turned in my brain as I nodded along.

"So, you know that your body has the ability to heal itself, right?"

I nodded again like a bobble head.

"When you cut your finger, you don't have to tell your body what to do to heal it. Your body just knows. It detects the injury and goes to work to send the correct cells to the area to form a clot, then it begins a healing process to repair the damaged area."

"Right," I responded.

"Okay, so that intelligence is called your body's innate wisdom. That is what I will be communicating with for your session. The way that I will do that is through a technique called neuromuscular biofeedback. Some people call it muscle testing. It will look something like this," she said as she touched my forearm.

"I will silently ask yes or no questions in my mind as I move through the BodyTalk protocol chart you see right here. Just so you understand how this works, a "Yes" answer feels very light to me. Your hand will feel very easy to move, whereas a "No" answer feels very heavy. "No" feels very hard for me to lift your hand. That is how I set up the muscle testing protocol."

"Okay," I agreed. *I guess that sounds okay.*

"And, try not to worry," she added, "If your arm isn't relaxed, the muscle testing won't work, so there is no way you can mess with the answers I receive from your body."

As she seemed to read my logical mind, my skepticism melted a little.

"So, all you have to do is lie there and relax. Feel free to close your eyes and focus on your breathing. I will just work silently, as not to distract you, then I will explain the details as they surface and, if required, will ask any questions to get further details."

"Okay. Sounds good," I added, feeling like a broken record.

"Now you can rest, relax, and pay attention to what you are feeling in your body or noticing in your thoughts. If there is anything trying to get your attention or popping into your mind, please feel free to let me know," she added.

"Okay, I will," I said, unsure if I would even be able to notice if my body talked to me. It was not that I didn't realize how I felt in my body. It was that I had never learned to listen to or value those messages.

To start, she led me through a relaxation visualization, which helped me quiet my mind, relax my body, and get connected with myself. While I focused on my breathing, she began using the muscle testing technique on my arm to communicate with my body's innate wisdom.

Innate wisdom, I pondered. *The internal intelligence that coordinates the healing of the body without conscious direction. Interesting.*

Wow, she's talking to my body, I thought. *You can do that?* I wondered, impressed, but skeptical.

She dove in deep right away and brought up some issues and emotions that she never could have known about me. Heck, I barely had any awareness of my own emotions. Immediately, said emotions bubbled up to the surface, and as I begin to blink them back, she encouraged me to let them flow.

"Emotions come to the surface to be released. Just let them roll," she said, smiling. "It happens all the time. Don't hold them back," as she handed me a Kleenex box.

What? Really? I thought, as I plucked a couple of thin hospital Kleenexes from the box.

As uncomfortable as I was letting people see my emotions, I tried to pull down my mask of holding it together, at least until the session ended. I had never felt comfortable discussing heavy emotions like fear and grief, but somehow, the practitioner helped me feel safe and comfortable in this new experience. I didn't feel judged. I felt understood and nurtured.

About halfway through the session, I really had to pee. Typically, I had a strong bladder, but the pressure of the tumour sitting on my bladder had rendered me powerless to the urge to run to the bathroom on a regular basis. "Sorry," I interrupted, "Can I go to the bathroom?"

"By all means," she replied. "Your body needs a release. That's totally okay."

I hobbled my way to the bathroom with my IV stand in tow. To my surprise, the blood in my urine that had been bright red just prior to starting the BodyTalk session was now barely visible.

Well, that is weird, I thought to myself, puzzled.

When I came out of the bathroom, I laid back down in the hospital bed and told the BodyTalk practitioner about the change. "All of the blood that was in my urine is basically gone," I stated with a look of disbelief plastered all over my face.

"That happens all the time," she said nonchalantly. "Your body is getting reconnected with itself, so it is better able to know what it needs to do to help you heal."

"Whoa," I said, wide-eyed. *What IS she doing?*

As the session continued, she brought up my maternal grandmother who had passed away almost exactly a year prior. Tears, that I hadn't been willing to allow out very often, began to surface. Soon after, my right ovary come up as a priority in the session, which meant it was requiring attention and rebalancing. Then it came up, again. And again. From what she explained, my right ovary required a lot of reconnection.

Huh, okay, I thought. *Whatever that means.*

She went on to explain that the ovaries represent the point of creation, creativity, and our connection to our own femininity.

Well, then. I'm not connected to any of that. On the contrary, I seem to reject those aspects of myself. That can't be a good thing, I thought, *but it sure makes sense.*

Upon completion of the session, I was in awe. My mind was completely blown. The information she conveyed during the BodyTalk session was so incredibly accurate. How could she have known all of that? I wondered in shock. She noted that everything that came up in our BodyTalk session was now balanced out by the techniques she had done.

When my parents returned, I said, with wide-eyed amazement, "The blood in my urine disappeared!" Knowing my stent surgery had been only 24 hours prior, they were also amazed.

How did that happen? I wondered, curiously. *There must be something to this.*

After the practitioner explained the session to my parents, they left together for Mom and Dad to have their own BodyTalk sessions. With so much new information to process, I valued some alone time as my brain attempted to make sense of the monumental experience.

My mind was blown.

"Cheers to all the people who can change their minds when presented with information that contradicts their beliefs."
– Unknown

My sports medicine brain had needed to see the physical proof for it to believe this holistic therapy could be helpful for me. That first session was just the beginning of loads of synchronistic proof presented from my bodymind that would continue to blow my mind, time and time again. Within the week, I had four more BodyTalk sessions—yes, five sessions within seven days.

What I learned about myself and the bodymind connection fascinated me:

- *Emotions can get stored in the body. What?! Those emotional holdings can disrupt the body's communication and functions?*

- *The body is an emotional filing cabinet? Wow.*

- *Active memories are past experiences that were not fully mentally processed, thus still hold an emotional charge and affect the bodymind? For real?*

- *My beliefs shape my reality. How?*

While I wasn't sure what I believed yet, I could not discount the healing I had witnessed and experienced within myself. And that was precisely what my scared ego needed—hope. Strangely enough, this new information resonated deeply within me and made a lot of sense to my logical mind. It was like I had been delivered a stack of lost puzzle pieces that snapped together to help the bigger picture slowly, but surely, come into view.

Never in a million years did I expect that cancer would lead me to such a drastically new perspective, and all within four days of diagnosis .

IT TAKES A VILLAGE

"We don't have to do it alone. We were never meant to."
— Brené Brown

Mom handled calling all of our family members and messaging some of my childhood friends and Mercyhurst friends. When you're from a small town, the word gets around pretty fast, and it didn't take long for the word to spread about the cancer diagnosis I was facing. Honestly, that was okay with me as it turned into an outpouring of support from even the most unlikely people and places. Phone calls, emails, and text messages flooded our phones. My windowsill quickly became filled with bouquets of flowers, cards, and hordes of stuffed animals. My hospital room had turned into a revolving door of my Mercyhurst besties, childhood friends, brothers, grandparents, aunts, uncles, cousins, family friends, and beyond. In moments of complete devastation, you have to give yourself permission to lean on others until you're able to stand on your own once again.

I enjoyed the visits as they helped me talk about what was going on in person, but they were a lot to take in. From relatives crying with my parents in the hallway to my closest friends trying to play it cool while choking back tears, the emotional reactions were intense, and it was a lot to process. Some people felt the shock when they first heard the news. For others, the reality flooded in and hit them like a tidal wave upon seeing the visual of me in a hospital bed. So, imagine bearing witness to the smack of that emotional wave at the exact moment someone lays their eyes on you. Talk about emotional overload for a girl determined to hold it together, when I really should have allowed myself to just be whatever I needed to be in each moment.

I was open and honest with what was going on—medically, anyway. I shared the news and wanted to openly communicate with everyone. I didn't have anything to hide. Honestly, I feel this was one of the best things I could have done. It might have been easier to hide, lay low, and not tell anyone the truth, but what good would that have done? I was carrying enough emotional baggage—I didn't need to carry secrets. Because my family was open in our communication, it opened the door for others to speak up, ask questions, and share their feelings, even if I didn't. It allowed my friends and family to feel safe visiting me instead of feeling awkward and emotional. I'm so grateful to the friends and family that took the time to stop by to see me. It might seem insignificant, but it never went unnoticed.

Some of my closest friends and relatives came to visit me often, and I cherished those moments so much more than they will ever know. I appreciated their courage in showing up. It can feel really uncomfortable to visit someone in the hospital when a scary diagnosis is lingering in the air. They were a safe haven—a comfortable place for me to land on to let go of my heavy reality.

I tried to show everyone how "okay" I was, which was pretty typical for me. Between cracking jokes and asking my friends how they were doing to divert the attention off of my situation, it seemed to help everyone feel more comfortable. All that meant though, was that I wasn't being honest with myself in just how scared I felt. Expressing emotion was uncomfortable for me, and that was fairly typical behaviour for me. Even as a child, I was always mature for my age. I sensed how others felt and was always the one friends came to for advice or to vent. So, when anyone asked me how I felt, my fairly standard reply was that I was doing, "not too bad."

I mean, come on. Not too bad? Really?

My best friend, Lindsey, or "Linds" as I called her, drove five hours to come to see me as soon as she heard the news. When she wasn't able to get time off of work at her summer job, so she quit to be there for me. Hearing that story come out of her mouth brought me to tears. Can you imagine something so important to you that you'd quit your job if your boss wouldn't give you time off? That's the definition of true friendship right there.

A few days later, Brittany—my high school bestie through the ups and downs—drove from Edmonton to see me too. She was adamant I would get through this. While she blinked back tears, she hugged me tight like she always did, and I knew without a shadow of a doubt she believed I'd be okay. I always admired her unwavering determination. She would state something with such conviction that everyone around her knew she would make it happen. If Brittany said it would be done, you'd better get out of her way, because nothing could stop her. That was the exact energy I needed to channel. Luckily, we had spent countless hours together throughout our toughest years, and I'd been marinated in her conviction, determination, and courage.

Kevin was my best guy friend from high school. He was basically the male version of me, and I the female version of him. We both cleaned up on the athletic awards from elementary school throughout high school and claimed spots on our high school Athletic Wall of Fame. Because he moved away for hockey in high school and I played intense club volleyball in the city, we were in a similar boat, athletically—living and breathing our sport of choice. Thus, we often missed out on the typical high school festivities and weekend shenanigans that all our friends talked about on Monday morning in class, which helped us relate to one another, and allowed our friendship to grow.

The first time Kev visited me in the hospital, he might as well have been bawling. He was fidgety, awkward, and terrified, and it was written all over his face. He brought me a boy band poster so I would have some "eye candy" to look at while I was in the hospital. While his gift was light and meant to be funny, his laughter didn't effectively hide his fear. To see him like that hit me right in the chest. We were both far too good at stuffing our emotions.

Meds, my best guy friend from Mercyhurst, visited me often. He was a steady friend who accepted me unconditionally. Whether it was our his Saskatchewan roots or his down-to-earth personality, there was something about him that brought a sense of comfort and an instant feeling of trust. His visits always brought laughter, comfort, and many good memories.

LIGHTEN UP

"Humor is the great thing, the saving thing after all. The minute it crops up, all our hardnesses yield, all our irritations, and resentments flit away, and a sunny spirit takes their place."
– Mark Twain

When I was hit with the cancer diagnosis, the tension between Mark and me subsided. Even though we'd broken up, he had been my best friend for almost two years. So, when shit hit the fan, he was the one I wanted to talk to.

He would have done anything for me. When I was in the hospital, he sat by my side every day for two weeks. If I needed anything, he would jump at the chance to go get it. He kept the hospital atmosphere light with his humour, offered to help at the drop of a hat, and brought me a bunch of goofy and unnecessary gifts in his attempts to cheer me up. One day he showed up with a nerf gun. He tore into the packaging, loaded it up, and handed it to me, insisting for fun to ensue. Gift giving was his thing. His jokes and childlike playfulness always helped to diffuse the tension and heaviness in the hospital room, which made way for laughter, healing, and loads of smiles. He helped my entire family far more than he ever realized.

I truly appreciated Mark's support, though there were times that became uncomfortable as I tried to keep our boundaries clear. Sometimes I felt frustrated and confused. *Why is he still here? Doesn't he know we aren't together?* But he didn't care. He wasn't leaving. I don't know what I would have done had our roles been reversed, but I truly admired and appreciated his dedication, courage, and unwavering support when I needed it most.

While things didn't work out between us, I learned so many important things about myself from our relationship. He taught me how I should be treated in a relationship—with respect, equality, consideration, and unconditional love. He showed me chivalry, which was a fairly foreign concept to me before we started dating. While I initially rejected his chivalrous displays to prove I was a feminist and could do it myself, I soon realized he was simply showing that he cared. He taught me commitment and how to be silly, to play, and to have fun. He was always joking around, pulling pranks on people, and laughing. Even though I rolled my eyes often, he taught me how to lighten up and not take life so seriously. In all honesty, I swear that was the key for me. As the well-known quote by Elbert Hubbard goes, "Do not take life too seriously. You will never get out of it alive."

When you live life so seriously all the time, every decision becomes stressful, every mistake feels like the end of the world, and you end up trying to live up to the expectations of others, often curating a life you "think" you should live. I never stopped to ask myself, "Am I happy? Is my life filling my soul? Is there anything I would like to change, adjust, or edit?"

Isn't that a lot of pressure?

GASTRO CLEAN OUT

While Dr. Giede was away, the other doctors mentioned that surgery would be booked for early in the week after he had returned, which meant that I had been mentally and emotionally preparing for that news upon his return. While all of the tests had seemed to be inconclusive, the mass needed to be removed from my body.

The night before my big surgery, a nurse brought me a giant, triangular-shaped plastic container filled with one litre of a drink that would clean out my bowels to prepare me for my surgery the next day. I had to drink it fully within an hour and a half.

Seems simple enough, I thought.

The container held a clear liquid with loads of ice. It had measurements on the side of it like a beaker from science class. I took a sip. Huh, not too bad. I thought. I'd be able to do this, no problem.

Boy was I wrong.

It didn't take long before the "not-badness" of this drink went south real fast as I realized the impending doom that was coming my way. Soon, I was choking it down with a god-awful expression on my face as the taste sent shivers through my body. The fear of how this drink would obliterate my bowels was likely why I began digging in my heels and making this experience much more difficult than it needed to be. Regardless, my mom wasn't letting me get out of this one.

My college friend, Christine, had come to visit that night. She sat with me as I choked the drink down and witnessed the enthusiasm and confidence drain from my face. She tried chatting to keep my mind off of the drink before heading home for the night. I had yet to still finish the drink.

"It's so gross. I can't drink it anymore," I said as the taste sent a shiver up my spine.

"You have to," Mom insisted.

"What can we do to help?" Dad asked.

"The ice is melting faster than I can drink it," I grumbled.

"Give it here," Mom said, as she took the container to the bathroom to scoop out the ice cubes and try to boost my confidence.

"What is she doing?" I asked Dad, hopeful that she was pouring it down the sink.

"She's getting rid of the ice," he noted.

"Ugh," I groaned, helplessly.

"Do you want to try chewing some gum while you drink it?" Dad asked with his eyebrows up. "It might be worth a try."

"I guess so," I replied reluctantly, and off they went to find me some gum; giving me a brief reprieve from the awful taste. The gum helped for all of thirty seconds, and then I was back to gagging the drink down.

As Mom left the room to ask the nurse a question, Dad said, "Come on, Toad. You can do it. It can't be that bad."

"Why don't you try it then?" I barked at him, my words laced with attitude. That sort of attitude was usually what I gave to my mom, not my dad. I was a Daddy's girl at heart, so he could tell I was desperate and out of patience. Understanding this, he got up from his chair and came to my bedside. As I wondered what he was doing, he grabbed the plastic container, brought it up to his mouth, and took a couple giant swallows.

My face lit up in disbelief, then a giant smile began to stretch across my face.

"Seriously?" I said with my eyebrows raised as high as they could physically go. "Whoa. That just happened," I laughed. "Now you're going to get the scoots like me!"

"Ahh, a little clean out juice never hurt anyone...just cleanses the tailpipe."

I don't know where my dad got his strange humour from, but it usually made me laugh for the simple fact that it always came out of left field. Sarcastic and unpredictable. With one eyebrow raised, I shook my head. I couldn't believe he'd just done that. He would have done anything to help me any day of the week but seeing me struggling pulled on every heart string he had.

"Now it's your turn," he said. "It's not that bad. You can do it."

I knew there was no getting out of it now. "Fine," I said, rolling my eyes. I raised the container to my lips, then paused to take in a deep breath and let out a big sigh before pouring the liquid into my mouth. I swallowed, and my entire body shivered.

"Quick, have another," Dad encouraged me. I obliged then shivered again, sticking my tongue out with a look of disgust plastered all over my face.

Dad peeked into the hall to make sure the coast was clear, and then he took a few more giant gulps of the drink. Now that's love right there.

When the intestinal Drano started working work its magic, my guts began to rumble and roll. What a terrifying feeling that was. *How serious is this going to be?* I had no idea what to expect, but the sounds coming from my intestines were audible to everyone in the room. I wasn't about to wait to see how this was going to play out, so up I got out of the hospital bed and wheeled my IV stand into the bathroom to set up shop. I wasn't leaving until this was over.

Just then, I heard my phone ringing. *Oh no!* Suddenly, I remembered that earlier in the day Matt (formerly known as Mr. Muscles) had said he would call to wish me well for my surgery. We had been keeping in touch over the summer, and while it was great he called, the last thing I wanted was for my dad to answer.

No, no, no. Please don't let that be Matt.

"Do you want me to get that?" Dad hollered.

"No, that's okay. Just leave it!" I yelled back through the bathroom door.

I heard footsteps walking toward the bedside table where my phone was plugged in.

Noooo, I yelled on the inside.

Either he didn't hear me or else he blatantly ignored my request—either were plausible explanations. "It's Matt Pierce," Dad said as he read out the caller ID. The timing couldn't have been worse. Of course, hunky Mr. Muscles would call while the cleanout drink was just about to take effect.

Please, don't answer it, I thought.

"Hello?" Dad said as he answered the phone and started talking to his future son-in-law—he just didn't know it yet, and neither did I.

The awkwardness was almost painful! I hoped so badly that Dad wouldn't say something embarrassing. As my intestines let loose, I knew there was no chance in hell that I'd be able to leave the bathroom until I was completely cleaned out. That damn juice really worked.

Let it go, let it gooooo.

As I resigned to my fate, I heard Dad tell Matt that I was in the bathroom, but that I would call him back later. I could feel my face turning six shades of red as I listened to their conversation through the bathroom door. Here was hoping they couldn't hear me.

THE DOCTOR IS IN

On my seventh day in the hospital, the doctor we had been waiting for finally stood in the hall outside my hospital room at Royal University Hospital.

"Is he here? Is that him?" we whispered to the nurse. Except my mom didn't whisper—I wasn't sure she knew how. It used to embarrass me a lot. "Mom, they can hear you," I'd say, annoyed. But, this time, it didn't bother me at all. She was relieved and excited.

"Yes, it is," the nurse assured us.

We had been waiting for this moment since arriving in Saskatoon. Dr. Giede was the gynaecological oncologist that could give us some details and the things we'd been waiting for the most—answers. We had been waiting almost seven full days to meet this man and the moment had finally arrived. We were ready to "go on the offensive" as my dad would say and get this dealt with.

He finally walked in, holding my chart, and introduced himself, "Hi there, I'm Dr. Giede." (pronounced G-ee-da). His voice was soft and on the quiet side; making me wonder if he was sheepish. His wire-rimmed glasses surrounded his gentle eyes. He was mostly bald and about forty-five years of age. He was here to tell us what they suspected was happening inside my body and what they planned to do about it.

"You've had stents put in, correct?"

"Yes, I have," I confirmed.

"Perfect. How are you feeling after that? Have you had any relief from the pain?" he inquired.

"Yes, my kidney pain is totally gone now and the blood in my urine has subsided, as well," I noted.

"Okay, great. So, what we've discovered is that you have a type of germ cell tumour called a dysgerminoma."

"Okay," I said, without a clue of what that meant.

"Can you spell that for me?" Mom asked as she scribbled notes on a notepad. She was ready to take notes with every doctor or nurse interaction, blood work, and test result. Nothing got past her. This was her super-strength—organizing, asking questions, and ensuring she understood exactly what was happening. She was smart as hell, and I admired those qualities in her. Luckily, I've always been on the receiving end of this super-strength, which she wonderfully instilled in me (with less intensity).

Dr. Giede tried to spell it off the top of his head, "D-Y-S," he paused and opened my file. "Yes," he continued, "D-Y-S-G-E-R-M-I-N-O-M-A.

"Thanks," Mom said .

"Dysgerminoma is a rare, but malignant, form of cancer. However, it is very treatable and responsive to chemotherapy, with a ninety per cent cure rate. We must confirm everything with the pathology report after the surgery, of course."

My parents and I looked at each other like we had just been given the best gift in the universe. My stomach settled, and I exhaled a sigh of relief. I hadn't realized that I had been holding my breath, nor that I was clenching my jaw and tensing my muscles. I took another deep breath and focused on relaxing my muscles. *Thank God.*

"That's great news!" Dad said.

"That's the best possible news you could have delivered!" Mom beamed.

"Because we have not been able to determine which organ is affected, we won't know what we are taking out until we open you up for surgery. However, the organ is definitely reproductive. So, we plan to do your surgery after hours as soon as we can book an operating room at City Hospital, which will likely be this evening."

"In the meantime, do you mind if I examine your abdomen?" he asked.

"Nope, not at all. Go for it," I urged. "It's grown quite a bit since I arrived at the hospital last Wednesday. They said I looked like I was twenty weeks pregnant when I was first admitted."

"Oh, okay," Dr. Giede said, pondering, as he pressed firmly on my belly.

After completing the exam and asking a few more questions, he explained his plan. "I plan to do an incision similar to a Cesarean section—nice and low on the abdomen," as he motioned to the location on my tummy. "It will be a small incision that will heal up nicely and won't interfere with your strong abs," he chuckled. I relaxed a bit and smiled.

"Because you are so young, we want to do everything we can to preserve your fertility. You probably don't know if you want kids, and we don't want to make you have to decide about that if we can help it."

"Uhh, yeah, I don't know," I stumbled.

Fertility? Geez. I guess I hadn't thought about the fact that I might not be able to have kids. At that moment, all I could feel was the continued embarrassment of talking about reproductive organs with my parents in the room. My family had never been open in communication about sexuality, so this felt awkward for me. However, upon looking at my parents, rather than looking uncomfortable as well, they just seemed relieved—happy that I'd still have the option. And thank goodness I *wouldn't* have to choose. All that really mattered right now was getting through this, . I was not even close to thinking about having kids, but I had always pictured being a mother, and it was nice the option would still be there for me.

"If one ovary is affected, we will remove it and leave the unaffected one intact," Dr. Giede continued.

Okay, I thought. *Makes sense.*

"If both ovaries are malignant, then we will remove the worst one and treat the other one with chemotherapy afterwards. You're too young to decide if you want kids and since this type of tumour typically responds well to chemotherapy, it's worth it to go that route, if necessary."

Whoa. Okay. Stop talking about having babies, please. I was still recovering from the pregnancy harassment comments before my CT scan. This is a lot to take in.

My mind skipped to chemotherapy. Ugh. We were hoping surgery would be enough and that I wouldn't need to have chemo or radiation. Clearly, the false positivity wasn't working.

"If your uterus is affected, which, I don't believe it is, then we must decide once we open you up about how to proceed. But we will do everything we can to preserve your fertility."

"Okay," I responded, despite drowning in information overload.

My parents asked questions and Dr. Giede did his best to answer. He was very thorough, and I appreciated his patience in answering the stockpile of questions that erupted from our mouths.

"So, will she need chemotherapy for sure?" Mom asked.

"We won't know that until after surgery. But I just got back from Ottawa where I learned about the advances in chemotherapy drugs. There have been a lot of improvements, but we will cross that bridge if we have to."

We nodded in unison. Mom asked for best-case and worst-case scenarios. Best-case: the tumour was contained, gets fully removed, and I don't need chemo. Worst-case: the tumour couldn't fully be removed and needs to be treated with chemo. Since the type was typically very treatable, even the worst-case scenario was much better than the real worst-case scenario I was avoiding in the back of my mind.

"Well, I hope you can get the tumour out easily, that it is contained, and that she won't need chemo!" Mom said cheerily.

Dr. Giede smiled as he heard Mom's comment, but I could tell he had a more realist-type of perspective after working in the oncology profession.

"The nurses will keep you updated with the surgery time at City Hospital and will get you prepped. I will see you over there." My parents thanked him, he nodded and headed out to proceed with his day.

My parents and I looked at each other with big, excited smiles. "YAY!" Mom squealed while dancing with her arms, the way moms do. They both hugged me and squeezed extra tight. We were all so damn grateful for this news. After we verbally and mentally processed some of what we'd just learned, Mom headed out to go make some phone calls and share the news.

We definitely weren't out of the woods, but it was a step in the right direction.

THE POWER OF A DIAGNOSIS

*"No person and no thing have any power over you
unless you give them that power."*
– Lynda Field

There were many times I had reflected on how "lucky" I was to have been given a promising diagnosis. However, I had decided long before Dr. Giede told us the news that I would not succumb. I was not going to die. I was all in and ready to do whatever it took, and my parents were on board too— even if that meant opening our minds to anything and everything that might help along the way.

With Western medicine, we are trained to believe we need to go to the doctor to be fixed with medicine. Now, this is a sweeping generalization, yes, but it rings true for the majority of the population of the Western Hemisphere. When I was younger, this was true for my family. We were taught that the doctor knew what was wrong with us and how to help us get better. That understanding isn't necessarily wrong, but there is an important distinction to be made: A doctor is human. A doctor is functioning from his or her level of understanding, consciousness, and awareness—just like we are. Doctors don't know everything—how could they? And how could we expect them to?

A doctor doesn't heal your body. Your bodymind knows how to heal and does so all the time without you even realizing. Doctors help support your body in healing when your symptoms are too far gone and your bodymind needs extra support. But, in Western medicine, doctors often treat the physical body, separating it into its parts. When we look at the body as a whole—physically, mentally, emotionally, and spiritually—it provides a new perspective on health. When we own the fact that we are the creators of our experience, we can peel back the layers that lie emotionally and mentally beneath the surface of our symptoms, revealing a powerful opportunity to heal, no matter the diagnosis.

Doctors have an incredible impact on the state of a patient's recovery or lack thereof. I can't even imagine how heavy that responsibility would weigh on the shoulders of doctors and nurses. But it is important to consider that diagnoses and prognoses are professional opinions. Sure, they are often well-educated opinions, but they are not gospel. No matter the amount of training doctors have, they don't know what mental programs you've been running on, what fears keep you up at night, how you are mentally and emotionally dealing with your state of health (or lack thereof), what stresses you out, nor the underlying triggers to all of it. Heck, we barely know these things about ourselves! How on Earth could they know? So, when we put all our faith in believing that a doctor's diagnosis is factual truth, then we hand over our healing power to the doctor. Sure, sometimes the odds fall in our favour. But other times prognoses can be grim, and when combined with a fear that immobilizes the immune system, the medical prediction can easily become our reality. The mind is that powerful. But, you get to choose how you respond.

Dr. Bernie Siegel said, "I see people who die a few minutes after a doctor tells them there is no hope of a cure. They give up and go. Others get angry and find joy in proving the doctor wrong. Something within them is challenged and hopeful. Hope is the divine motivator." How powerful is that?!

You are a whole package. Your mind, body, beliefs, mindset, and emotional baggage all are huge factors that affect your physical health, yet the physical body is often the piece of the puzzle that is treated. Do you see why we need to take prognoses with a grain of sand? Doctors do their best with the information they have available to them. But, when we only look at a few pieces of the puzzle without taking into account the mental and emotional aspects of the bodymind, it can make it pretty darn hard to accurately predict the outcome.

I do not say this to place any kind of blame on anyone. Everyone is doing the best they can. However, physical symptoms only give a small piece of the whole story happening within you—and those symptoms are what western medicine then treats. There is so much more to this story than the physical body. And that is what I found out the hard way.

The point I'm trying to get across here is quite simply: Please don't fully hand over your healing, your health, or your fate to a doctor, but instead see your doctor as part of your support team. When you can take ownership of your experience, then you also assume the power to change it. This does not mean you won't need help. This does not mean you won't need medical aid from western medicine, eastern medicine, or alternative healthcare available to you. What it does mean is that you don't give someone else the power to tell you if you're going to live or die. Owning your experience is the key to healing. If you can take ownership—rather than blaming 439,285 things outside of you for your experience—then you can begin the internal work that will create healing within your body and mind. *That* is a powerful place to be in.

THE BIG DAY

"Something will grow from all you are going through.
And it will be you."
– Unknown

It was June 27th, 2007. I was scheduled for a 6:00 p.m. surgery at City Hospital in Saskatoon. The day of pre-surgical fasting crawled by as my stomach growled for nourishment. After being transported to City Hospital, I changed into an unflattering, pale blue hospital gown and anxiously sat in the pre-op waiting room with my parents.

Tension crackled between us as we nervously sat amongst the other strangers. We did our best to support each other and stay positive as we went blindly into this surgery, with no clue as to what to expect. What do you say when awaiting a major "life-altering, change-everything" type of surgery? I put on a brave face and was as ready as I would ever be. At least we would have some answers after this. All of this not-knowing business was starting to weigh on me.

When my name was finally called, the nurse brought me a wheelchair, which I thought was unnecessary, but I obliged. My parents hugged me, then I climbed into the silver-wheeled chariot. I tried to smile and blinked back the tears pricking the backs of my eyes. *It's going to be okay,* I reminded myself. *Deep breath.*

"We will see you in a few hours, Miss," Mom said.

"It's going to go great, Toad," added Dad.

The surgery itself was scheduled to last four hours. But when the doctors are going in blind, you never know what could happen. I hoped they were right.

Not knowing what to say back, I kept quiet. *How am I supposed to act at a time like this?* I wondered. I couldn't bear to show my parents (or more importantly, myself) just how scared I truly was. *Positive mindset,* I reminded myself. *You've got this. And your doctors have got this.*

We weaved through the halls and the nurse delivered me to the door of the operating room. It looked like any other hospital office door, which I thought to be strange. There was nothing significant or remarkable about this door, yet it was the entryway to my next dimension of healing.

The operating room was filled with a natural, bright light, emanating from the wall of windows that looked out to a lush landscape of bright green grass and trees. In Saskatchewan, the summer sunshine keeps our corner of the world bright until 10:00 p.m. or later, which was one of my favourite things about summer. Seeing something so colourful and so tied to many of my childhood memories, helped calm my nerves.

I climbed up onto the surgical table, laid down, and further inspected the room while I waited. My sports medicine nerdiness instantly kicked in, helping to distract me for a few moments. Memories of the three orthopaedic surgeries I observed at school popped into my mind, and I remembered how relaxed and enjoyable the OR atmosphere was. I pulled from those experiences; calling that sense of calm to me. *I wonder what music the doctors will listen to tonight.*

The anesthesiologist asked me a question, bringing my focus back to the reality that I was the surgical patient this time and not an observer. I chit-chatted with Dr. Giede, the other surgeon, and the nurses in the room, which lightened the mood and put my mind at ease before the anesthesiologist sent me off to la-la land.

My brothers had planned to join my parents at the hospital to help pass the time and provide emotional support while I was in the operating room. While my surgery was underway, Kiel and his girlfriend, Chantel, joined my parents after work and Kenton planned to stop at home for a quick nap before reporting to the hospital. The hours passed and when Kenton didn't reply to any calls or texts, the others started to wonder what was going on. Eventually, at 10:00 p.m., just as my parents found out my surgery had been successfully completed, Kenton called to say he had laid down for his "quick nap" at 6:00 p.m. and woke up *four hours later*—which just happened to be the exact duration of my surgery. I mean, what are the chances that my adult brother would have a four-hour evening nap? He hot tailed it to the hospital and made it before I got out of recovery.

We were all blown away by the synchronicity of the timing. My brother slept the *entire* duration of my surgery. And while my over logical family would have normally sloughed this event off as a random coincidence, it became obvious that our minds had begun to open up. Thanks to BodyTalk, we were starting to see the connection between the mental, emotional, and physical realms. We were all being impacted and opened up to new awareness and learning that we had never considered before. And because of that, we all grew together while witnessing the magic that can happen when stuck between a rock and a hard place.

Bright lights and the sound of beeping monitors flooded my awareness as I slowly woke. My eyelids felt as though they weighed a thousand pounds each; just opening them took all the energy I could muster before they would collapse shut again. A nurse appeared at my bedside to tell me that I was in the recovery room. I felt groggy and mildly confused, until my memory refreshed and my mind began to connect the dots.

When I tried to speak, the words wouldn't come out the way I intended them to, as though my body and my brain weren't totally plugged into one another. Time felt very distorted as I drifted in and out of sleep. I could sense nurses moving around me, but my whole body felt like it was being pulled into sleep by the force of gravity—and I couldn't resist. Before I knew it, I was surrounded by my parents, Kenton, Kiel, and Chantel who were all talking to me and squeezing my hand.

"Hi, Miss. We are here with you, now. You made it out of surgery."

"Hi, Toad. You did great, just like we knew you would."

"It's all behind you now," Kiel said with encouragement.

"Good job, Kristin," Chantel added.

"Hi, Sis. I'm so glad you're okay," Kenton said as he wiped his eyes.

I tried to smile, but everything was so foggy. I faded in and out of consciousness, while hearing the conversations happening around me. As I attempted to open my eyes again to look at them and thank them for coming, I could see they all had tears in their eyes. Gratitude washed through all of us knowing that surgery was officially behind us.

Sleep pulled me back under until I felt my bed moving again. I was being wheeled up to a hospital room as Dr. Giede joined my entourage to debrief us on what they discovered and how the surgery went.

"The surgery went well. We removed a five-pound, football-sized tumour. It was the right ovary and fallopian tube that were affected. We also had to remove a lymph node by the aorta of Kristin's heart. All of the other lymph nodes were clear and the tumour was contained. Because we needed to inspect the lymph nodes, I had to make the incision longitudinally from the pubic bone up and around the navel, so it is quite a bit bigger than I had initially anticipated. But it allowed us to make sure we didn't miss anything."

In my anesthetic haze, my mental processing had some major lag time. "Does that mean I will only get my period every other month?" I inquired. Everyone laughed, thinking I was making a joke to lighten the mood. *Why are they laughing?* I felt it was a legitimate question. I only had one ovary now—didn't that mean I should only have my period every other month?

Dr. Giede could sense my hazy confusion, so he broke it down for me. It turns out, the body was extremely adaptable. So, in my case, with the removal of one ovary, my body said (in what I imagined to be a GPS voice), "Recalculating..." and my left ovary picked up the slack.

WHOSE BODY IS THIS?

"The scars you acquire while exercising courage
will never make you feel inferior."
D. A. Battista

That night that anesthetic haze continued to consume me as exhaustion overtook every cell of my body. It felt like I was living in a fuzzy dream world. The night went by in a flash, and upon waking up I felt off kilter. My mind felt foggy as I attempted to get my bearings. Every move sent a shockwave through my body as I became aware of how traumatized my body was.

The next morning, the nurse came in to check on me. She showed me how to support my stomach if I needed to move. Using a folded-up blanket, she placed it lengthwise, following the direction of my incision. "Apply some gentle pressure through the blanket to support your tummy," she instructed.

I was hesitant, as I was scared to even touch my stomach, but I gave it a try. The pressure felt like a relief as it eased my nerves and the feeling of being vulnerable and helpless. I still didn't want to move, but this new trick helped to relieve the extreme apprehension I felt about moving or the possibility of a cough coming on.

Have you ever considered *how much* you use your abdominal muscles? It's literally all the time for every movement that you make. But, just like any other body part, you don't realize this until the affected location hurts every time you attempt to use it. As I slowly tested the waters of this new state of my body, it became clear that I had greatly unappreciated how much my abdomen had supported me for my entire life. My pain was under control so long as I didn't move. Suddenly, I became intensely afraid of breathing too deep or coughing, I noticed that laughing made me wince, and I felt as though a sneeze might blow my abdomen wide open.

As someone who had been physically capable of pretty much anything, this was a very uncomfortable condition to be in. *Who was I without a strong, muscular abdomen? Who was I without my independence?* My abdomen was completely useless. In order to sit up, I had to carefully raise my hospital bed using the automatic controls, then use my arm to cautiously pull myself onto my side, while bracing my abdomen with a folded-up blanket as to not place direct pressure on my incision. The amount of energy that it took to sit up was almost unbearable.

Then, the nurse picked up a bag that was attached to my bed. I could feel a twinge of a burning sensation. The bag was full of a yellow fluid. Slowly, my brain put two and two together.

Whoa. That's pee! Wait, I thought. *Is that mine?!* That explained why I hadn't had to get up to use the bathroom. The nurse mentioned that they wanted to remove my catheter by the end of the day and get me up going to the bathroom by myself.

My eyes widened in horror. *What? No!* I panicked on the inside. *I can barely sit up, let alone get out of bed!* The thought of having to get up to go to the bathroom that was right beside me evoked severe anxiety. It seemed like I begged Mom to ask to keep the catheter in a bit longer. Never in my life did I expect to be begging to keep a catheter, but in that moment, getting to the bathroom on my own with my entire abdomen sliced down the middle felt like an impossible mountain to climb. The nursing team agreed to leave the catheter to calm my post-surgical anxiety, when I agreed to do my best to get up and moving.

Next, the nurse proceeded to redress my incision. As she peeled back the bandage, everything moved in slow motion. It felt like I was staring down at someone else's abdomen. Twenty-six staples and ten visible stitches grasped the left and right sides of an abdomen together with all of their might. I felt the blood drain from my face as I gazed down at a body I did not recognize. The twelve inch incision began above my belly button, then traveled down and around it, through my navel piercing hole, and continued down my lower abdomen past my Hawaiian flower tattoo to my pubic bone.

"Dr. Giede did a great job," the nurse said.

I was reeling. *That's my stomach.*

Even though I had heard that the incision was big, and it also felt like my abdomen had been physically obliterated, nothing could mentally or emotionally prepare me to see my body in this state. I didn't understand it. *How can this be my body?* The wheels began turning as I mentally processed the information that I could recall from the night before. Now, coherent, I attempted to fit the pieces of my new reality together like a jigsaw puzzle, but I still wasn't able to fully grasp what had happened.

Questions flooded into my mind, but I held them in until the nurse left. Unleashing them the moment she did.

"Why did they have to do the incision this way again?"

"Because they had to check the lymph nodes by your heart," Mom said. "They removed one."

I struggled to process what that meant. "And how big was the tumour?"

"It was five pounds and the size of a football." Mom could see my wheels turning. "Why don't we ask Dr. Giede to explain everything again when he comes in to check on you."

"Okay," I agreed, even though I was left reeling in the midst of the emotions that were flooding me.

Later, Dr. Giede re-explained what he had told my parents the night before. "The surgery went as well as it could have. Your right ovary and fallopian tube were affected, and we also had to remove a lymph node by the aorta of your heart. Because we needed to inspect the lymph nodes up here," he said as he pointed higher on my abdomen, "We had to make the incision longitudinally from the pubic bone up and around the navel. That is why it is quite a bit bigger than I had initially told you it would be. But it allowed us to make sure we didn't miss anything. You have about twenty-six staples and ten stitches, and I even added some permanent sutures to make sure everything holds together well for you, so you'll have your strong stomach back in no time," he smiled.

Whoa. The information hit me much harder this time around.

Dr. Giede elaborated on the dysgerminoma. "We have sent the tumour off to the lab for testing so will know more once we get the pathology report back. We think the tumour was stage three, as it had already spread to one lymph node. Once we can confirm, we will know how to proceed."

Damn. As if I didn't have enough processing to do, the now possibility of chemotherapy had been added to the pile. I was overloaded. I'd had been so used to believing I was strong, athletic, and healthy that my whole persepctive of self was crumbling before my eyes. My devastating reality was starting to

sink in. *How could this happen? Where did I go wrong?*

DON'T BE A HERO

When I awoke from surgery, I had been hooked to an intravenous morphine drip. It came with a button that I could press when I needed another dose for pain management. The button itself was moderated so that I couldn't self-administer too much of it. By the time my anesthetic fog had begun to lift, I had already been regularly scratching my face. When I was more coherent and aware, I was still unable to control the urge to itch.

"Stop scratching," Mom said. "Why are you doing that?"

"I'm so itchy!" I told her, "I can't help it."

Because the morphine made me feel like a drug addict, I only pressed the button when it was absolutely necessary—which was before I had to move, sit up to eat, or reposition myself.

My body didn't respond well to pain killers. If the meds were able to relieve the pain, they did so with a very negative side effect that accompanied the relief, as if to serve as self-punishment for not being able to handle the pain on my own. That physical reaction was not surprising considering I believed I had to be strong all the time—that mentality didn't exactly match up with the acceptance of pain relief support.

That night, as Dr. Giede and the nurse came in to do their rounds, the nurse quizzed me with a hint of concern in her voice. "Why haven't you been using your morphine button?" It was twenty-four hours post-op and I hadn't realized that I'd barely touched my button that entire afternoon. It wasn't intentional, but the itchy side effect was barely worth the pain relief it provided. Plus, I wasn't really in pain unless I moved. All eyes were on me as they awaited my response.

"Umm..." I stumbled, confused, "Because I don't have any pain unless I'm moving," I finally said.

It was true. Since my first BodyTalk session, Mom and I had been doing a brain-balancing technique called "Cortices" that was meant to calm the brain, ensure coordination between the left and right hemispheres, and balance the brain's communication with the rest of the bodymind, which then reduced pain and symptoms, while promoting healing. Clearly, it was working!

"You don't have to be a hero," the nurse said, with a look of disbelief plastered all over her face.

Whoa. Really? Is that what they say to all their patients?

I frowned. "I'm not trying to be a hero," I answered. "It really doesn't hurt. I use it when I have to move. But otherwise, why would I use it if I don't need to?"

The doctor and nurses couldn't refute my logic, yet they still seemed quite unimpressed. They could not wrap their heads around why I wasn't having any pain. I, on the other hand, was quite pleased. The BodyTalk sessions were helping me learn how to reconnect with myself, and it was time to start speaking up for myself. A sense of pride filled me and I smiled.

I began to understand that just because the medical professionals expected my body to do, feel, or act in a certain way didn't mean that was an accurate expectation. Clearly, no one had believed my initial symptoms anyway, so it was time I started to learn how to trust my body first and foremost, regardless of what anyone else had to say about it. For once, I wasn't trying to be a hero—I was finally listening to my body.

CREAM OF (NO) POTATO

It is my understanding that for the surgeons to ensure they didn't miss any of the tumour and to properly check lymph nodes and inspect my thoracic cavity, they removed my intestines from my abdomen and placed them on a stainless-steel cart beside the operating table. This also explained why I had to drink that lovely clean out drink—they needed to be able to fit my intestines back into my abdomen afterwards. Crazy, right?

In the days following surgery, I was on a very slow introduction to food while my body was attempting to navigate its new intestinal path. The first day post-op, my diet consisted of clear fluids such as soup broth, apple juice, and Jell-O—all of which could be sucked up through a straw. But, damn, it tasted good to have nourishment hit my lips. Considering I hadn't eaten anything substantial since before the dreadful gastrointestinal cleanse, it had been almost seventy-two hours without a real meal, and I was famished. Hunger pangs did not even begin to describe the sensations my stomach sent to me. Luckily, I had a fair amount of distractions, such as attempting to move in any way after having my abdomen sliced open.

By supper time, I frantically searched for a piece of potato that had made it past the strainer into my bowl of cream of (no) potato soup. But, no dice. Damn. I'd never been so hungry in my life. I groaned in desperation, and my stomach rumbled in agreement.

"I'm *so* hungry," I dramatically told my parents. Cream fluids just weren't cutting it anymore. It felt like my stomach was eating itself from the inside out. I was starving.

"What can we do?" my parents asked. Many times, I didn't know how to answer that question. We had a stash of snacks in my hospital room, which normally would have been my saving grace between hospital meals if my appetite would have been normal. But, nothing in our snack stash would have been safe enough for me to try during this stage of recovery.

"I'll go for a walk to see what I can find," Dad said. He would have done anything under the sun to take away my pain. Mom would have, too. And they both were gutsy enough to go rummaging around the shared kitchen to sneak me some food.

When he returned, the clouds parted as he held in his glorious hands a cup of Easy Mac. "Will this work?" he asked.

"YES! YES! YES!" I exclaimed! It wasn't exactly a cream liquid, but it was close enough. Right? So, off he snuck back to the kitchen room to prepare the Easy Mac. I had never been so excited to eat before, and I couldn't contain my sheer enthusiasm for the relief that was on its way. My mouth watered, and my stomach growled like a starving puppy whining for its supper.

When Dad returned with the bowl of comfort, I carefully tested a bite, then another. It was the best thing I had ever tasted! Okay, probably not—let's be serious—but, the relief was next level. As I lied in the hospital bed about to shovel my third bite of cheesy noodle magic into my mouth, the doctor and nurse walked in. My eyes grew wide and I immediately froze.

Busted.

SHE'S SO FLUFFY

With the possibility of chemotherapy lurking over my shoulder, I did the logical thing and begged my parents for a puppy. I figured if I was going to be doing a whole lot of nothing for the majority of the summer, I might as well have a little companion to play and snuggle with. Truthfully, I never thought my dad would cave on this one, but I figured it was worth a shot. He was a logical dude, so if anything would get him to soften his mind on his permanent no-pets stance, it would be the possibility of chemo.

Growing up, Dad had always instantaneously kiboshed our hopes and dreams of having a four-legged pet. Instead, he opted for birds as pets—canaries first, then a lovebird, and then finches.

I grew up with the sound of our canaries' sweet and sunny melodies as the background soundtrack to my home life. Those cheery songs could brighten even the darkest of days.

Can you imagine singing all the time, no matter what? Talk about a mood-lifting pet.

When I was in grade three, Mom and Dad went on a Caribbean cruise to St. Maarten and a bunch of other tropical islands. The souvenir they brought home was a peach-faced lovebird, named Koko, who instantly became our prized possession. She rode on our shoulders, hung out just under the collar of our shirts peeking her head out, and sat on our fingers. My brothers built her a perch with K'Nex that attached to a remote-controlled car. She would sit on the perch as my brothers drove her around the basement. What a cool pet!

However, when it came to dogs, cats, or anything with four legs and hair, the response was always a hard, unwavering "No." It seemed easier for people who have never had dogs to easily discount the comfort, healing, and companionship they provide.

Asking for a puppy became my obsession after surgery. I had been a frequent visitor to the pet store at the mall in Erie. A mini pinscher had first stolen my heart, but it was the faint memory of a small, fluffy puppy that I knew was the one I wanted. However, I had no idea what breed of dog it was. So Mark, being the kind of guy that he is, took it upon himself to serve as my research assistant. He would Google various kinds of small fluffy dogs and would bring me printed pictures and breed details until he eventually found "the one".

When I laid my eyes on the picture of a tiny, fluffy puppy, I was so excited! YES!! I excitedly, yet carefully, wiggled my legs as much as I could without injuring myself. My face was lit up and my eyes flooded with brightness!

"It's a toy Pomeranian," Mark said.

"OH! She's so fluffy! I want her! Look how stinking cute she is!" I said as I held my hand under the picture.

THE SPACE BETWEEN

"Honour the space between no longer and not yet."
– Nancy Levin

After my ten-day hospital stay, I was triumphantly released from its sterile confines. My oncologist told me to go home and recover while we waited for the pathology report to deliver our next course of action. Once again, I had my own personal chauffeur to escort me, via wheelchair, to the main entrance of the hospital.

Like a ninety-year-old, I delicately climbed into the front seat of the vehicle while Dad helped me awkwardly pick up and place each leg inside the car. Once settled inside, he slowly reclined my seat as Mom gently placed a pillow over my abdomen before buckling up my seatbelt. And just like that, I found myself homeward bound once again. Only this time, in a much different state; physically and emotionally.

The ride home was exhausting. I felt every bump, pothole, and crack in the road as the movement jarred my fragile body. I tried to let my exhaustion whisk me away to sleep, but it only resulted in a few cat naps between potholes. When we pulled into the driveway at home, I was relieved to make my way to the stationary couch; to no longer be bounced into fatigue and muscle soreness.

While at home in Rosetown, I cautiously traveled from my bedroom to the bathroom to the couch. Mom mostly waited on me, but the nurses wanted her to encourage me to get moving. The fastest way to help my body heal was to use it and build up my stamina again. Mind you, I had to do so with a delicacy that I had never had to apply to my life before. Considering I had always been a full-blown athlete who gave 110 percent, taking it easy was not necessarily in the repertoire of my skillset. I had some learning to do, and most importantly, I had to keep listening to my body.

My stamina had deteriorated quickly after living in a hospital bed for two weeks, so I tired easily and couldn't be outside soaking up that Saskatchewan summer sunshine for too long without feeling completely drained of energy. As a result, I was forced to rest, a lot, and take it easy because I had to—if I did too much, my body would let me know via extreme fatigue, incision issues, and total body soreness. Despite it all, anytime I was feeling "okay" enough, I focused on having as normal an experience as possible. Because more than I needed rest, I so deeply craved a little glimpse of normalcy—to have a break from my harsh reality and the common pitying looks of "having cancer".

One sunny afternoon, Kevin and his mom stopped by for a visit. I was close with his parents, and they had visited me multiple times while I was in the hospital. Every time I saw his mom, emotions flooded through me and I found myself blinking back tears. It was obvious in her eyes that her son had been having a hard time with the news and she was doing her best to support him through it. She was always so cheery, encouraging, and positive, and I loved her for it.

Even though Kev and I were best friends, our communication just plain sucked. We both wore the mask of "being tough" far too tightly, which made it nearly impossible to open up about anything that weighed heavy on our hearts. This dynamic made it even more difficult to attempt to have a normal conversation while side-stepping anything real that was going on for either of us, emotionally.

As Kev and I sat in the living room, our moms' kitchen conversation filled the air, while we made small talk. We both wore plastered forced smiles on our faces and shoved our emotions out of sight. *Why do we do this?* I wondered as we mostly sat listening to our mothers talk amongst themselves, until the phone rang.

"Sorry, I have to take this," Mom said, "We've been waiting to hear from Kristin's oncologist," she explained as she excused herself to answer the phone.

We continued our conversation, while my mind wandered to the news Mom was receiving. We had been waiting for the pathology report to determine my next course of treatment, hoping that there wouldn't be any more treatment at all. Even though I had two weeks to wrap my head around the possibility of chemotherapy, I was mostly in denial as I hoped it was a dark road I wouldn't have to embark down. So, when Mom called me into the bedroom to tell me that the pathology report confirmed Dr. Giede's initial assessment, that they had removed a five-pound, football-sized, malignant, stage three germ cell tumour, I was not surprised...until she said that I needed three rounds of chemo. In an instant, I felt like I had been sucker-punched by the news. I was terrified and disappointed.

"Okay," I said to Mom while my throat tightened. As tears filled her eyes, she hugged me. In shock, I robotically hugged her back as I blinked back my own tears. My mind instantly turned to Kevin and his mom sitting on the other side of the wall in the living room. *What do I say? How should I act? I need a moment.*

Mom went back out to our guests while I went into the bathroom, pretending I had to pee. It felt like my chest had just been crushed by an elephant. It was so hard to breathe. I craved to hide out in my room to bawl my eyes out, but all I could think about was that I needed to hold it together for Kev. I knew he was having a hard time and I couldn't bear to let him see me crumble, even though it probably would have helped us both unpack some of our emotional baggage.

Get it together, Kristin, I told myself.

I returned to the living room with the front of "business as usual". While Kev's presence usually brought a sense of comfort, my despair was almost too much to hold. I was teetering on the edge of an emotional collapse while I internally begged for his departure. The weight of my emotions was almost too much to bear, but I didn't dare let my poker face slip. I couldn't stand to let my biggest supporters be filled with doubt and fear after seeing how defeated I felt. In hindsight, I wish I would have had the courage to lean on them.

Chemo, hey? Well, shit. This shouldn't have been surprising news, but I had been holding out for a miracle that I wouldn't need chemo at all. When Dr. Giede had said that I would likely need chemo, I clung to the doubt in that statement—the chance that I wouldn't need it. *He didn't say for sure, right?* So, when the confirmation came, it sucked the air from my lungs all over again.

How can this be my life? I wondered in desperation. I had a mountain of a journey in front of me—the toughest expedition in the most challenging of conditions—and it felt impossible to be positive about it. The terror was painful to fathom, and the questions rolled through my mind like an endless internal dialogue. *What will it be like? What will chemo feel like? Will I be sick all the time? What is it going to do to my body?* My head felt like it was going to explode as a headache began to form behind my eyes. My neck tightened, and I found it difficult to see the positive side of this situation. Everything looked so grim. I felt like I was full to the brim with emotions and attempted to do everything in my power not to spill myself all over the floor. It was a full-time job just trying to hold myself together. I wish I would have known that I didn't have to.

My mindset had been groomed through years of elite athletics. The words "mental toughness" echoed through my head in my coach's voice. It reminded me to pick myself up and carry on without letting my emotions toss me around. And while feeling down and being hard on myself never led to any place worth going, I had no idea what to do with the onslaught of emotions I was drowning in. Mental toughness was probably an unhealthy coping mechanism since I didn't learn how to come back to those emotions to work through them. Emotional processing was completely foreign to me. I'd never learned that having emotions was part of being human.

But just like I'd always done, I decided to stop feeling sorry for myself and gear up for the road ahead. *Chin up, buttercup.* I heard in my mind. Eventually, I set my eye on the prize of making it through the heart-breaking reality of chemo so that I could get back to school, my friends, my team, and finish my degree. To stick to "the plan" and stay the course gave me a goal and a sense of stability as I bobbed helplessly in an ocean of despair. This goal kept my head above water, while I kept my eyes on the finish line.

NERF GUN

In the days that followed, my body remained weary and overloaded with its healing agenda. Although I was one-week post-op, my staples were not ready to be removed yet, and I could barely move in any typical manner I once took for granted. The simple act of getting off the couch had me barrel rolling onto all fours on the floor, to then moving into a standing position. And even that exhausted my body, let alone other minor amounts of movement. So, I was sequestered to either the couch or my bedroom to rest and allow my abdominal muscles time to heal.

It was during one of those afternoons, when I was lying on the couch after lunch, talking on the phone with Mark and minding my own business, that I felt something smack me in the leg. Then the elbow. And then right in the head. What the hell is that?!

Just then, I saw a nerf gun bullet bounce off the couch and land right beside me as I took another hit in the hand that held the phone.

"Seriously?" I said as the anger started seething from me.

I looked over to find my twenty-year-old brother, Kiel, standing there with a shit-eating grin on his face. He was home on his lunch break from working at the tire shop. He wore a blue work t-shirt and old jeans that covered in grease marks and he smelled of rubber as he proudly shot his recovering sister repeatedly with a nerf gun.

Umm, are you kidding me right now?!

"Screw off!" I barked at him. "What the hell are you doing?! MOM!" I yelled furiously.

Yes, I was tattling. What else could I do?! Clearly, my grown-ass brother could not understand the severity of the incision that split my abdomen down the pipe. I could barely move to defend myself and that was the part that pissed me off the most. I was livid.

"Kiel is shooting me in the head with the nerf gun!"

"Relax, Kristin. It's not a big deal," he said, rolling his eyes at me.

Mom came over and scolded him, "Kristin just had major surgery. Why would you do that to her?"

"It's not a big deal. I was just messing around," he replied like water off a duck's back.

Mom had a perfectly timed aha moment, as she turned toward my brother, "Have you seen Kristin's incision yet?"

He hesitated. "No," he said sheepishly.

"Come over here and take a look," she said.

I lifted my shirt to reveal my padded gauze bandage and Mom helped me slowly peel it back to expose the harsh reality of a four-hour abdominal surgery. My brother stood beside the couch with reluctant anticipation. The faint blood-soaked bandage hit him like a freight train.

It wasn't pretty.

A twelve-inch incision occupied my abdomen from my pubic bone up the center, around my bellybutton, and beyond. Twenty-six staples held the left and right sides of my abdomen together. Ten sutures were knotted with meticulous placement amidst the staples. Beneath my war wound and invisible to the eye laid numerous permanent sutures for added support.

My brother's expression instantly turned to shock as the blood drained from his face. He looked as though he had just seen a ghost.

My anger softened as I looked at my brother. I could see it in his teary eyes that he had not expected my abdomen to look as raw and obliterated as it did. No one could have expected any of this. It felt so strange to be what my brother was looking at when his face had paled.

"This is why you cannot mess around with her," Mom said with a gentle voice, but a stern look in her eyes. "Any sudden movements could reopen her incision and could be very serious."

"I'm sorry," he said, as he blinked quickly.

"It's okay," I replied.

Mom said to me after he left, "I realized that your brothers probably hadn't seen your incision, and it made me wonder if this didn't seem real to them. You and I have been in the thick of all of this, so it didn't even cross my mind that they might not realize the severity. He needed to see it. We will show Kenton the next time he's home."

I nodded. "Well, he successfully fulfilled his brotherly duties of being annoying."

It was this memory that really highlighted the fact that, even though I was the one in the hospital bed, I wasn't the only one that had been impacted that summer. We were all forced, in our own way, to navigate that devastating health crisis.

Mom was with me through the thick of it all. Through every needle prick, blood test, palpation, doctor appointment, blood transfusion, swipe of the hair clippers, exploding vein, and bag of chemo drugs—she was right by my side. Sure, she wasn't physically being poked with the needles, but she might as well have been because emotionally and mentally, she was being put through the exact same ringer as me.

Dad was in the hospital with us most of the time, and I know his heart broke with each test, poke, and medical interview I had to endure. He also came with me to one of my chemo sessions, and even though he was always a trooper who rarely showed his emotions, I sensed that the reality of it all smack him hard that day.

My brothers didn't come to chemo, which I later found out was because Mom wanted to protect them from the harsh reality of it. But that didn't stop them from getting a backstage pass to the traumatic experience when they joined us in the hospital, at the lake, at home in Rosetown, or in Saskatoon.

"Do you remember shooting me with a nerf gun?" I asked my Kiel, as we chatted on the phone during one of my writing breaks.

"What? No. Seriously?" he asked, surprised. "Well, I guess that sounds like something I would have done back then," he admitted, laughing.

"Yeah, I was lying on the couch at home after getting out of the hospital. You were on your lunch break and you started shooting me repeatedly. Oh my god, I got so mad. But as I was writing the chapter, I realized..." A lump formed in my throat. "It was your way of showing that you wanted me to be okay." Tears welled up in my eyes. "You just wanted your sister back," I squeaked. "You wanted me to be able to goof around with you so that you'd know I was going to be okay."

The line went silent, then his voice croaked, "I'm really glad you made it through that summer."

"I know," I smiled. "I am, too. Thank you for being there."

NOTHING TO BLAME

"When you pass the blame instead of owning your experience,
you give up your power to learn, grow, and change."
– Kristin Pierce

Attempting to make sense of a cancer diagnosis was wildly confusing. Not having anything to blame was the greatest gift that could have ever come from an experience with cancer. I couldn't settle with blaming cancer on reasons x, y, or z and carry on with my life because even the doctors were flabbergasted. Being in sports medicine, the reality of cancer didn't line up with my understanding of health, and I wasn't about to sit back until I got to the bottom of this. *Why? Why is this happening to me?* Questions continued to roll through my mind. Luckily, I was a headstrong girl who would not give up until I found some understanding.

As I continued to have BodyTalk sessions, I began to see just how much I was holding in emotionally. I rarely expressed how I felt, verbally or visibly, and I began to realize just how unhealthy that truly was. My BodyTalk practitioner opened my eyes to the fact that we are so much more than physical beings. While this logic didn't completely align with my schooling and understanding of the body, somewhere inside of me this truth resonated to my core. As much as my logical mind had a hard time swallowing this truth, it couldn't deny it. I had to know more.

Every session, I eagerly awaited what my practitioner would dig up from the depths of my consciousness. And every session, the accuracy of the information that she brought to the surface blew me away. Things I didn't even realize I had been feeling came up in a way that resonated so deeply within me that my logical mind couldn't refute it. After all, there was no medical, logical, or physical reason for me to have cancer at such a young age, especially when I was so physically healthy—and thank goodness for that. Not having a logical reason for cancer opened my mind and led me on an eager quest to discover the root cause. I desperately craved understanding, even if that meant I had to widen my perspective and take ownership of my experience in order to find it.

Blaming something external for our experience allows us to pass the buck. Blame means we don't have to look at the part we play in contributing to our personal experience. Blame puts a person in victim mode, and no healing can ever be done from that state-of-being. Now, this doesn't mean go lather on a heavy dose of self-blame, either. Nope, not for one second. Flinging the mud of self-blame at yourself is not even remotely similar to taking personal responsibility for your experience.

Oprah said, "True forgiveness is when you can say, 'Thank you for that experience.'" This statement also applies when the person you most need to extend the olive branch to is yourself.

DIESEL

There is nothing truer in this world than the love of a good dog."
– Mira Grant

After much debate, Mom was convinced that it wasn't such a bad idea for me to have a puppy as a healing companion.

WHAT?! Really?! I was so surprised. I didn't think there was even a sliver of a chance they would actually let me get a dog. I guess Mom had enough logic to back her argument to Dad, because soon enough she was Googling Pomeranians available in Saskatchewan. YES! My masterplan had worked, and little did my parents know, the dog would help them more than they could ever anticipate.

One morning at the lake, while Mom sipped coffee and I relaxed on the couch in my pyjamas, Mom and I looked through puppy pictures she had been emailed. An exorbitant number of "Awws" and "Oh my Gods" followed. The little Pomeranian fluff balls were so darn cute!

"Oh, look at this litter," Mom said, turning the computer my way. "They were born on May 13th! Lucky thirteen! It's a sign."

As you know, thirteen was a lucky number in our household—I was born on March 13th and a mere fifteen months later, my twin brothers were born on June 13th—so the birthday of this litter was a lucky sign for us, especially at a time like this.

In the litter of Pomeranians, there was one pup that was all black. She was so adorable that just looking at her photo made my heart want to burst. "Aww, I love this one," I said.

"Oh, she's so cute. Okay, I'll see if she's available." Mom said, as she started to type her reply.

Once the breeder confirmed the puppy was ours, Mom asked, "What are you going to name her?"

Hmm...What am I going to name her? I wondered.

I always felt that words and names held immense meaning. Her name would have to be meticulously deliberate, so I went down to my bedroom with a notepad and pen to reflect upon my soon-to-be-pup and the reminder of the strength I'd need through the challenges that undoubtedly lay ahead . She was small, but mighty. And I knew she would symbolize strength and comfort, so I wanted her name to be strong to match. I typed "strong dog names" into Google and compiled a list of possible names that might fit the bill for this bundle of cuteness.

On the list, there was one that stood out. Diesel. That was it. I pulled up her picture. "Diesel," I said out loud. Yep, that's her.

I started my slow, but excited ascent back up the stairs carrying my notepad.

"So, what'd you come up with?" Mom asked.

"Her name will be Diesel. She's going to be strong, fierce, and brave—even if she doesn't look like it on the surface." Just like me. She'd be the reminder I'd need through these next few months; this sweet, healing, companion pup.

"Diesel it is," Mom smiled.

Ten days later, we were off to North Battleford to pick up Diesel—our new family member and my healing companion.

We got home and Mom got Diesel and I settled in the living room. At first, my brothers seemed reluctant and unimpressed as they watched Mom help me and my new puppy. Their looks made me feel like a spoiled brat, but they didn't understand what it felt like to have nine weeks of chemo in front of me.

My Cosmic Hammer

Soon the front door opened, and Dad walked in after work.

"Shhhh! The puppy is sleeping," I whispered from the couch.

"I'm not being quiet for no damn dog," he stated strongly.

It took less than a week for Diesel to find her way into Dad's heart.

My brothers warmed up to her not much longer after that. This was never a moment we got to experience when we were little, so the inner child of each of us was bursting with excitement. Plus, she was just too damn cute not to love with your whole heart.

And just like that, we were all hooked.

THE CANCER CENTRE

"It is okay to be brave and afraid at the same time."
– Brené Brown

A week after the phone call from Dr. Giede, Mom and I headed to the city for an appointment about my upcoming chemotherapy program at the Saskatoon Cancer Centre. But as we pulled up near its front door, my stomach was twisted full of knots, and my mind was racing. *Breathe, Kristin. It's going to be okay.*

Walking toward the front doors felt as though everything was happening in slow motion. The doors opened automatically, inviting us inside, when I actually wanted to turn and run in the other direction. Goosebumps covered my body as we crossed the threshold into the building and were hit with the blast of air conditioning. I was beyond terrified to begin this next stage of treatment, no matter how much I tried to logic myself through it. To no fault of the Cancer Centre, it just had a weird feeling—an emotional intensity—if you will. My hands turned to ice, my spine tightened, and my body started to shiver. The fear ran high within me, and I knew I wasn't the only patient there feeling that way.

It must have been obvious that it was our first time there because the receptionist walked us through her step-by-step speech of where to go and how to get there. Was it my deer-in-the-headlights look or my mom's false positivity that gave us away?

We carefully followed the receptionist's directions down the hallway. I felt like a mouse in a maze. The hallways seemed to stretch into eternity, and I kind of wished they would have. That way, I could've escaped from the terrifying reality that was laid out before me. As we walked, the halls wove through the building and created a sense of confusion. Even though the waiting areas were all clearly labelled, a sense of uncertainty seemed to loom in the back of my mind. Never had I felt so awkward and out of place.

We rounded one corner, following the signs for blood work, only to find the chairs fully occupied. It felt as though every set of eyeballs turned to stare at us, and I instantly slammed it into reverse and retreated back the way we had come and found a spot at the end of the blood work hallway to sit. As fear coursed through my veins, I shook and blinked back tears, struggling to keep it together. After what felt like an eternity of waiting, the nurse called my letter. I walked through the hallway of doom and into the safety of the blood work room. No one stared at me in there. The nurse routinely confirmed my name and birthday, then proceeded to draw up my blood, filling vial after vial.

"Press here," she said as she removed the needle from my arm. I obliged as she sealed and labeled each vial of blood, added them into a canister. She tightened the lid, then stuck the canister in a vacuum delivery tube that fast tracked the vials to the lab.

"You're good to go," she mentioned, barely making eye contact. The nurses moved like robots through their routine, talking to each other as if the patients were barely there.

"Thank you," I noted as I stood up and walked out the opposite side of the blood work room. It was like a one-way street. Since there was so much traffic and so few parking spots, they funnelled patients through in one direction to ease the inevitable congestion of immuno-compromised humans. I looked around trying to get my bearings and was able to find our seats from earlier. Collecting Mom, we moved down to set up camp in Waiting Room C.

Which door is Dr. Giede's office? I wondered. As I sat in the waiting room, my stomach dancing with nerves, I tried to distract myself and breathe. Each time a door opened, I'd watch a nurse emerge, call a patient's name, and then take their weight before showing them into a room. I began to understand how this process would go. To help ease my nerves, I played a silent guessing game where I would attempt to predict which office door would open next.

"Kristin Peterson." My name was finally called, four doors and two correct guesses later.

"Hi Kristin, my name is Kathy. I'm going to be your chemo nurse," she said with a big smile and bright eyes, which was such a breath of fresh air.

"Come on in and have a seat. Mom, on the chair; Kristin, you can hop up on the exam table."

Kathy was in her fifties. She was dressed in nursing scrubs with a sweater over top and white tennis shoes. She had the sweetest, most understanding voice that made me feel instantly at ease, which was so necessary in a place like this. Kathy was the kind of person you just wanted to hug, knowing she would just make everything feel better. In an instant, I knew it would all be okay.

I relaxed my shoulders and jaw. *It doesn't feel as cold in this room,* I thought. Or, perhaps Kathy had helped me set down some of my fear. She was the sweetest soul I'd ever met in the hospital, and I was so grateful that she would be part of my team while I was there. Kindness and empathy seeped out of her—in her eyes, her voice, her body language, and her heart. I felt seen, understood, and heard just by her presence.

Kathy began a chemo debrief with us and explained how the process would go. She had a folder for us with various coloured pages full of information. I knew Mom would be very grateful for that and I was too. Medical meetings always seemed like information overload—it was just so much to take in, especially when survival mode was in full force.

"Kristin, you will have three cycles of chemotherapy, each being three weeks in length. You will receive chemo intravenously for five days in a row from Monday to Friday, then have the remainder of the three weeks off for recovery. That cycle will then repeat two more times."

Chemo will begin at 10:00 a.m., and on Mondays, you will have blood work at 9:15 a.m. before proceeding to chemo. Dr. Giede is only here on Wednesdays, so we have scheduled your appointments for that day too, to monitor how you're doing," Kathy said with her big, understanding eyes and her positive smile.

Mom took notes in her notebook and asked her typical ton of questions—all of which Kathy answered thoroughly and confidently. Then, while we waited for Dr. Giede to come in, Kathy described how chemotherapy will affect a patient's body.

CHEMO 101

"Tough times don't last. Tough people do."
– Unknown

"When it comes to chemotherapy, fevers are very serious. When on chemo, your body is waging a war. The chemotherapy will hunt and kill cancer cells, but it will also kill off many other healthy cells in the process because the medication cannot differentiate cancer cells from healthy cells. This means your body's immune system will be working on overdrive. When a fever spikes, it shows that the body is having a hard time keeping up with fighting off an infection or is struggling with the internal war. Either way, the first rule of thumb is: absolutely no Tylenol. We don't want to hide or mask the fever because it is a key indicator that something serious is happening internally. When a fever spikes, keep a close eye on it and report to the ER if it ever surpasses thirty-eight degrees Celsius." Kathy said, handing over the folder for us to look at as she spoke.

"Okay, no Tylenol. Got it," Mom said as she drew stars around the words *NO TYLENOL* in her notebook.

"Here is the phone number for the emergency room. If you do have to come, call ahead and tell them that you are one of Dr. Giede's chemotherapy patients. They will get a hold of either Dr. Giede or myself, but also feel free to call and leave a message on my answering machine if it is after hours. Here is my email and my direct phone line. Call me anytime."

"Next, hydration is important. One way the body rids itself of waste—whether that be cellular waste, toxins, etc.—is by water. You'll want to make sure you keep your fluid intake up to help your body with the process," Kathy said, looking at me.

"Okay," I said. "I can do that."

"Blood work is the key that earns you a rite of passage into chemotherapy. Your blood counts have to be good enough before you are permitted for chemo. If your counts ever drop, then chemo must be delayed, and we want to avoid that if we can help it. Because chemotherapy is targeting all of your cells, we need to make sure your white blood cells, haemoglobin, and platelets have enough surplus for your immune system to go to work."

Mom and I nodded in unison, "That makes sense," I agreed. I appreciated being able to understand what was going to be happening inside my body during chemo. This helped to calm my nerves as my anatomy brain appreciated and understood the logical information.

The doorknob turned and we all looked over in anticipation as the door swung open and Dr. Giede entered the room. "How are you doing today?" he asked with a slight smile and in his soft-spoken voice. He wasn't an overly emotional man, but I still felt comforted by his presence.

"Oh, not too bad," I replied with my standard response. Truthfully, it was one of the hardest days of my life so far, but the knot in my stomach and the panic in my nervous system had eased up a little.

"Kathy is just filling us in on everything," Mom told him.

Dr. Giede looked at Mom with her pen and notepad on her lap—a sight he had seen often in the past month. He smiled. "And Mom's keeping track of it all."

"I sure am," she replied, feeling proud that he noticed.

"Let's have a look at your incision," Dr. Giede said.

I laid back on the exam table and lifted my shirt to expose my abdomen. "That's healing up nicely," Dr. Giede said. "I did my best to not mess with your tattoo, and I'd say I did a pretty good job," he noted, smiling and proud.

"That's looking great," Kathy added.

"She got the rest of her staples out last Friday," Mom noted.

Have you ever had a doctor look at you with fatherly pride? It seemed as though I got glimpses of that with Dr. Giede. It wasn't all the time, but it sometimes happened when he let his guard slip and we got to have a peek at the big heart underneath the white coat.

"So, like I mentioned on the phone, the tumour was a stage three germ cell tumour called dysgerminoma. We did completely remove the tumour, along with the lymph node by your aorta, but the standard treatment is three rounds of chemo to make sure that we got absolutely everything, and you never have to deal with this ever again," Dr Giede explained.

"Recent research shows that of the three chemo drugs utilized for treatment for germ cell tumours, the harshest drug is not any more effective than the first two drugs on their own. That third drug has since been dropped from the routine, which is great news because it was the one that brought on some pretty awful side effects—like vomiting and hair loss."

"That's great news," Mom said.

"So, I won't lose my hair?" I asked, surprised and excited.

"The other two drugs are milder in terms of side effects on the body, so there would be a very slim chance of losing your hair."

"What percentage are we talking?" I asked.

"Well, it's hard to say for sure how your body will respond to the chemo, but my best guess is about a 10% chance it will fall out and a 90% chance it won't," Dr. Giede reassured me.

Oh, thank god. Thank you. Thank you! I thought. What a relief it was to hear those words.

"Do you have any other questions for me? If not, I'll let Kathy finish up with you guys and will see you next week," Dr. Giede said.

"No. Thank you," Mom and I said together.

We turned our attention back to Kathy as Dr. Giede left the room; allowing her to continue filling us in on her "Chemo 101" talk.

"Your white blood cells will bottom out at day ten of your cycle, meaning that the counts will be the lowest on that day. To help your body get back into the swing of blood cell production and to curb this low, we will be giving you doses of GCSF (granulocyte colony-stimulating factor) which stimulates blood cell production within the bone marrow. This dose will be given by subcutaneous injection—just a short needle in the thigh or the abdomen. We do need to keep the blood counts monitored since everyone is different and we don't know exactly how the body will react. These injections will start on day eight for a total of four doses." Little did I know how critical this little vial would become for my body.

"Lastly, you will need to take daily supplements when you're on chemo. The first is iron pills to support red blood cell production because the body will need lots of help. So, you will need to take three iron pills every day. Then, because iron pills can cause constipation, you will also need a stool softener. Anti-nausea meds will help to keep your nausea under control, and then Vitamin C will help support your immune system, as well."

While I felt light years better than I had when I'd first walked into the Cancer Centre, information overload was setting in. I had a lot to process, but all in all, I was given some pretty great news. I took a deep breath and let out a nice, long exhale. My hair will stay, I don't need the worst chemo drug...I can do this. I'm going to rock this. There is no other way. My spunk was restored.

Mom quizzed Kathy on all the details of the meds: brand recommendations, time of day to take the pills, and insurance. She then told Kathy that we were also doing BodyTalk sessions. Mom was proud to share how much the sessions had been helping me and wanted to make sure my oncology team knew about it.

"You guys do whatever you need to in order to support Kristin's healing," Kathy replied. And that is exactly how an oncology team should respond—with full support.

ARM CANDY

"True friends are the ones who show up with open arms,
no judgment, and no expectations, ready and willing to hold you up."
– Kristin Pierce

Before chemo began and much to my surprise, my friend, Landon, asked me to be his date to a wedding. Was it a pity date? Probably. But I didn't care. He was a good friend who happened to also be a total babe. He was tall, dark, and handsome with piercing ice-blue eyes. He had a strong, muscular build with impeccable posture. He oozed confidence, and he had a strong energy that matched his jawline.

I became friends with Landon when I was in grade seven and he was in grade ten. While there was something about him that made me feel mildly intimidated, I had also had a bit of a crush on him. He had never asked me on a real date before, so my long-time high school crush dreams were finally coming true.

In my quest to have a normal-ish existence before the shackles of chemo would soon attach themselves to my ankles, I desperately wanted to go. I so badly needed a breath of fresh air. Even though I knew that I would need to be cautious and listen to my body, I was at a point in my recovery where my staples had been removed and I was healed enough to make it through an evening's festivities without crashing too hard. The timing couldn't have been more perfect.

My Cosmic Hammer

After talking it over with my parents, which felt more like me repeatedly saying, "Can I go? Can I? Can I?" I was sure they could see how badly I needed to have just *one night* without the realness of "all things cancer". Since my parents and Landon's had become good friends, it helped everyone feel more at ease with me going to their lake. My parents agreed—with conditions of course since the reality of cancer could never really go away until the ordeal ended.

When arranging the details, Landon asked if I would want to go to his parents' cabin for the day on Friday, then travel together to Saskatoon for the wedding on Saturday. Since my uncle's surprise birthday party was planned for Friday night and was just a short drive from Landon's lake, it worked out perfectly for me to do both. As much as I was looking forward to some time away from my usual surroundings, I was still nervous. The enormous scar on my abdomen was still healing, which left me feeling self-conscious. Plus, I knew I had to be careful not to overdo it. Truthfully, I didn't want to be a Debbie Downer, but I guess Landon knew what he was signing up for when he invited me. I appreciated that he wasn't scared off by my circumstances, considering I was scheduled to start chemo the following week. His gesture in itself overwhelmed me with gratitude and left me appreciating him and our friendship more than I'd ever anticipated.

When I got to the lake, Landon was patient, gracious, considerate, and offered to help without me saying a word. I had never seen this side of him before, and I wasn't sure how to respond to it. He was well aware of how independent I had always been, so having his help and attention focused on me made my cheeks feel flushed.

When we decided to go to the beach, I went to the bathroom in his parents' cabin to carefully change into my bathing suit. I checked my gauze to make sure it was sealed tightly around my incision. The last thing I needed was to get sand in it. As I finished putting on my cute one-piece that conveniently covered my scar, I took a look at myself in the mirror. *Thank God for this bathing suit,* I thought. It was a cute little number, which helped give myself the allusion of confidence in a time where I wasn't feeling confident in the frail body I was sporting.

Walking on the beach with the feeling of sand between my toes therapeutic, but the exertion of doing so proved far more exhausting than it had ever been before. Finding a good spot to set up camp, we set down our towels, sun screened up, and laid down to get some vitamin D and rest. As I looked down at my body, I realized just how much it had changed. Where my luscious glutes used to spill out, they now barely existed—all deflated and flat. My strong arms had faded to bones with sinewy muscles hanging off of them. My flat, six-pack-abs had vanished, leaving behind a little protruding belly with a giant scar down the middle. Shrunken thigh muscles now hung from my femurs. My muscular body type had faded to skin and bones. I felt self-conscious and uncomfortable but tried my best to not let it ruin my day. Instead I choose to soak up the sun and good company.

After the beach, I headed to my uncle's nearby surprise birthday party where I got to spend time with my family, cousins, and family friends. Landon stayed at the lake and we agreed to meet up the next day. The majority of the chit chat with my family was about how I was feeling and healing up, which I was used to talking about by that point, but it was just so nice to attend a family get-together for a celebratory reason, rather than in a hospital room.

My cousin said, as she slid up next to me with an impressed look on her face, "So, I hear you're going to the wedding with Landon?" I knew she would have heard about it and wouldn't let it pass without commenting.

"Mmmhmm," I said proudly, sporting a huge smile.

I honestly didn't care if it was a pity date. I would have some good-looking arm candy, and that was just what the doctor ordered. The relief of a night out to act my age and focus my mind on something other than my health would be wildly good for my soul. To dance and be surrounded by strangers who wouldn't look at me with copious amounts of pity would be like coming up for air after an eternity underwater.

The next day, Landon and I casually cruised to the city in his car, pumping the music and blasting the air conditioning. Sitting still wasn't the most comfortable position, so I reclined the seat a little to take some pressure off my abdomen. Nothing was going to ruin my day, and the smile on my face was proof of that.

When we got to Saskatoon, we stopped at my brothers' university house to get ready. I slowly emerged from the car and let my body adjust to back into an upright, standing position before moving towards their house. As the heat of the sun touched my skin, I knew I had to get inside. Fatigue was already catching up with me.

Landon's chivalry continued as we went into the house to get fancied up and don our wedding attire. Gathered my outfit, I headed into the bathroom to change. Only, I'd run into a problem: my incision was oozing. Panic washed over me.

While the majority of the scar was healing nicely after the staples had been removed, there remained one small problem: the spot on the scar where the incision had been made through my belly button piercing was being a little pain in the ass. Because of the scar tissue, it was taking its sweet time healing up. So, as I peeled back my gauze, I saw a tiny hole in my abdomen. *Did a scab get pulled off? Was I sitting for too long? What the heck? Where does that hole go? I thought with a disgusted look on my face. And what do I tell Landon?*

I called Mom, frantic. "Mom, I have a hole in my incision!" I said, my voice laced with concern, as I stood in the bathroom whispering into the phone, hoping to God that Landon couldn't hear me. I'm sure my panicked voice did not make Mom feel relaxed or at ease. Once I elaborated and described that the hole was from my piercing, she helped me calm down and told me to just keep an eye on it.

I redressed my scar with a little extra padding and stuffed some gauze packets in my purse for safe keeping. The last thing I needed was to have my incision leaking through my dress at a wedding. *Eww.* I decided I had to be honest with Landon in case I had to ditch the wedding dance for any reason. So, I mustered my courage and turned six shades of red as I awkwardly told him my incision was oozing, noting that I might have to take it easy.

"Alright. That's fine," he replied calmly, with not even a hint of a reaction in his voice. I was taken aback with how unphased he was by my vulnerability. *Huh,* I thought. And that was that.

I ended up knowing a few people at the wedding, most of whom ended up getting completely loaded, as I sat back and watched the show. I had a couple of drinks but had no intentions of having any more than that. Since I didn't drink at all in high school, all of my friends were used to me being more of a designated driver than the drunken life of the party. Plus, whenever someone asked to buy me a drink and I declined, I had cancer card in my back pocket that would shut anyone up in an instant. When drunken acquaintances are convinced you need a drink, desperate times call for desperate measures. No one had the guts to question that reasoning.

By the end of the night, one friend in a drunken haze wanted to have a real heart-to-heart as he supported himself by holding the railing. "All you do is take care of your body and all I do is abuse mine, and you get cancer. It doesn't even make sense," he said with his eyes half-closed, his body swaying from side-to-side.

You're telling me, man. I don't get it either.

Throughout the entire night, Landon was a perfect gentleman. He introduced me to the people he knew, he graciously waited for me during the times I had to check my incision so I wouldn't get lost in a sea of strangers, and he always took the time to ensure I was doing okay and felt included. He never once made me feel like I was holding him back from having a good time. I was able to just enjoy the night as Kristin, not someone recovering from surgery and preparing for chemotherapy.

It felt nice to have a break from being "sick", and having Landon as my chivalrous arm candy was definitely a boost for my confidence and, thus, my immune system. It was just what the doctor ordered.

BUZZ CUTS

"There is no pain greater than to be helpless
in the face of a loved one's suffering."
– Unknown

On the weekend before I started chemo, I came upstairs to find my brothers with freshly shaved heads.

"Looks good, you dorks!" I said, rubbing their stubbly heads.

"Wasn't that nice of them?" Mom asked.

Huh? I wondered with a look of confusion. At first, I had no idea why they had done it. I literally could not connect the dots of how my brothers' new haircuts had anything to do with me. But Mom's comment made me realize that they had shaved their heads for me.

Why did they do that? I wondered, puzzled. *Don't they know I'm not going to lose my hair?*

Since Dr. Giede had told me that my hair wouldn't fall out, I was actually kind of confused by this gesture of support. But my brothers' wide smiles beamed bright enough to light up the room. I gave them hugs and thanked them, still mentally processing the gesture.

In hindsight, there was a subconscious display of foreshadowing happening that I now know I was deeply resistant to acknowledging at that time.

"Let's get a picture of you guys," Mom said.

We all stood in the kitchen and smiled. My brothers were visibly excited to sport their new dos. This experience was affecting them too, and shaving their heads was their way of showing me support as I entered this next phase of treatment.

I appreciated everything my brothers had done for me that summer, even by way of sitting around, playing with Diesel, and watching TV with me—giving me the normalcy I craved. Their presence and support was comforting and their twin shenanigans was always entertaining. I was sure they felt helpless too, and perhaps they shaved their heads to show me they were sitting in the fire right alongside me. For all of it, it meant a lot to me.

ON THE FIRST DAY OF CHEMO

"Courage is being scared to death but saddling up anyway."
– John Wayne

I was terrified when my first day of chemo arrived. To know that you are on your way to have your body pumped full of chemicals that will kill cancer cells along with all other types of cells in your body wasn't exactly relieving. As much as I understood that chemo would ensure I wouldn't have to deal with cancer again, every part of me wanted to run away and hide.

I tried my best to maintain my composure, despite my frayed nerves. It probably would have been good to talk about and honour my feelings, rather than holding everything inside and leaving it to pile up. But I was in survival mode, and to admit fear seemed to equate an admission of defeat. So, I put on a brave face and tried to keep my mind on the optimistic route.

Only three rounds of chemo. Five days, on then two weeks off. I can do this.

The knots inside my stomach grew tighter as we drove into the city. While I understood that chemo was the logical course of action, that realization didn't ease my racing mind and nervous gut. Questions looped nonstop through my mind. I attempted to take deeps breaths, knowing full well that Mom could sense my nervousness. And maybe, I could sense hers too.

As we pulled into the parking lot, we parked in the spots designated for Cancer Centre patients. It felt eerie to realize we got to take advantage of these close parking spots. I didn't want to have to park here. Ugh. My throat tightened, and my armpits and palms grew sweaty. My pecs were outrageously tight as I realized I'd had my arms clamped down by my sides for the entire drive into the city (heart protection at its finest).

As I walked in through the back doors into the Cancer Centre, chills ran up my spine as the air conditioning once again smacked me like a freight train. *Brrrrrrrrr.* I walked stiffly to the reception desk to check-in. My spine tightened, and my hands turned to ice.

"First day of chemo?" she asked, nonchalantly.

"Yep," I offered a fake smile that I'm sure she had seen hundreds of times over.

She reminded me where to go first. "You can go to blood work first, then proceed to Waiting Room C."

"Thank you," I replied as Mom joined me at the counter.

"Please ensure to sanitize your hands before heading into the appointment area," she added.

Mom led the way, since she could tell I was having a hard-enough time keeping my teeth from chattering. Was I cold or was I scared? Was I cold because I was scared? Fear surged through my body with an intensity you'd find in a horror movie.

We followed the long maze of hallways that I, once again, wished would stretch into eternity. The waiting areas were all clearly labelled as we proceeded to blood work. I took a plastic letter and we sat down, awkwardly. I exchanged slight pity smiles with the other people waiting around us while questions rolled through my mind: *Why is she here? He looks young. Which one of them is sick? Is that a wig? Does everyone lose their hair? I hope I'm not going to look like a "cancer patient".*

As I glanced around, my gaze met with numerous people who eyed me up. *Where do I look?* I didn't want anyone to think I was staring at them. Clearly, these people were all in the same boat as me. My stomach flipped and I looked up to the ceiling, blinking back tears as if I was trying to convince the tears to roll back into my eyes. While these questions moved through my mind, I realized that others probably looked at me and wondered the same things. *She looks young. I wonder what's wrong with her.*

I distracted myself by silently guessing who would get called next for blood work and did the math to figure out how many people were ahead of me in line. Whispered conversations were still overheard by everyone else in the waiting room, and we all waited (not so patiently) and listened for the nurse to call a new letter.

"Breathe, honey," Mom reminded me.

"Do I see Dr. Giede today before I start chemo?"

"No, not today. We will go straight to chemo for 10:00 a.m.," she answered.

I felt tense. My nerves were on red alert. *I'm not ready for this,* I thought.

After what felt like forever, the nurse called my letter for blood work. I stood up and walked with an outstretched hand—in what felt again like slow motion—to deliver the plastic letter while trying not to trip on my own feet. My hands were like ice as she drew up my blood work before directing me to Waiting Room C. By now, I'd had so many needle pricks, it didn't even bother me to watch the needle get pushed through my skin and watch the blood spurt into the vial. I guess I had gotten used to it.

We set up camp in the next waiting room anticipating the lottery call of my name.

"You're the next lucky contestant on cancer patient Monday!" Nothing about this felt fun or relaxing. I felt cold, shivery, and tense. I've got this. I've got this. I tried to convince myself. Soon, my name was called, which disrupted my mind's racing thoughts. We followed the nurse into the uncharted chemotherapy area.

I walked in with my mom like a scared child going to a new daycare for the first time—wide-eyed and taking it all in wondering, "You're not going to leave me here, are you?"

We passed the pharmacology desk and followed the nurse as the hallway angled to the right. Lining each side of the hall were small chemo rooms—each with a reclining chair, a side table, and a big window. As I looked into the rooms we passed, I saw cancer patients reclined in the chairs, covered with blankets—some sleeping, some chipper—as the beeping sound of the IV machines pumped chemo into their bodies.

The nurses bustled about with happy tones and cheerful smiles.

"Good morning," one nurse said as she opened a large metal door and pulled out a blanket.

"That is our blanket warmer," said the nurse we were following. "One of the best parts of being here is getting a nice warm blanket whenever you want," she said as she smiled.

How can they be so happy? I wondered.

We walked to the end of the hall and were shown into a room on the left.

"This is where you will be today. Afterwards, and for the remainder of your chemo sessions, you'll be down in one of those rooms with a recliner that we walked by."

Looking around, it looked more like an oversized hospital room with a bed. The fluorescent lights made me squint in discomfort. They were annoyingly bright and in no way did they induce relaxation or a feeling of comfort. And even though the room had a big wall of windows that looked out onto the greenery towards the South Saskatchewan River, it didn't help incite any calm.

I sat down on the bed as the nurse explained everything to us. It continued to happen in slow motion, except this time, the kind of slow-motion where the sound was distorted and you couldn't make out any of the words. The reality of chemo hit me like a sack of hammers. It felt all too real. I watched the nurse put my IV in and tape it on my skin—seeing it all happen as if I was an onlooker viewing it all from outside my own body. She hooked up a bag of saline, pushed a few buttons, and then the fluid made its way into my body. The noises of the IV machine sent chills up my spine.

A bag of saline, then a small bag of anti-nausea meds, followed by two chemo bags and more saline, I recited in my mind.

"Try to relax and rest," the nurse said kindly. "I'll bring you a couple of blankets, then I'll be back when your saline is done to change the bag."

"Thanks," I said emptily, forcing an obviously fake smile back in her direction. It wasn't her fault I was here. With my mind and body feeling full of fear, I was abnormally quiet. There were no words to describe how I felt in that moment, so I didn't bother, but I wasn't pretending I was okay. Already, I felt emotionally drained and physically exhausted, and it was barely 10:30 a.m.

Mom asked if she could tap my cortices. She could sense that my mind and my body could use some assistance in preparing for this healing process. "This is going to ensure that you never have to do this again, Miss," Mom said, reminding me of why we signed up for this treatment.

How you perceive chemotherapy can greatly affect its effectiveness inside your body. To help shift my mindset, I first needed to get my bodymind out of survival mode. Otherwise, the healing and survival modes would clash like oil and vinegar. The cortices technique would help me to calm my brain and restore communication between the hemispheres, which can initiate the body's natural healing process. It's amazing how quickly the body can heal when we get our emotional baggage, expectations, and limiting beliefs out of the way.

Once the saline and anti-nausea meds were done, it was go-time. This was the part I had been dreading. *Breathe, Kristin.* Chemo was the insurance we were told I needed to 100% ensure that I would never have to deal with cancer again.

The nurse hooked the chemo bag up to my IV and pushed the start button. The buzz-like sound of the IV machine started its rhythmic pumping as it pushed the medication down the tubing toward my bloodstream. Tears began to pool in my eyes. My throat tightened. My chest felt heavy and my shoulders rounded in. Vulnerable did not even begin to describe how I felt in that moment. I held my breath in anticipation.

Breathe, KP, I reminded myself as I watched the drip continue to fill with chemo until I couldn't handle it anymore. I tossed the blanket over my arm and rolled toward the window where I finally let my emotional baggage spill open as the tears ran freely across my cheeks.

On day two, I was introduced to the rooms with recliner chairs. They were just big enough to house a recliner, a couple of plastic chairs, and an IV stand. A wall of windows looked out to the green landscape of the University of Saskatchewan campus—giving me something else to look at. With each subsequent day of chemo, little by little, my nerves settled as I got used to my new routine and counted down the days to freedom. Each day, I battled the emotions of sadness, grief, and fear, while trying to remain positive and hopeful, which was a challenge in itself. Emotions would hit me like the tide out of the blue when my energy and courage reserves ran low.

On day three, I learned that every Wednesday a local business provided free pizza. As the aroma of cheesy goodness wafted through the Cancer Centre, my mood lifted. *Yes, I want pizza!* It was a lovely distraction from my gloomy reality.

By the end of day three, my body began to puff up like a soggy bowl of mini wheats. With two and a half litres of fluid being pumped into my body every day, it was no wonder I started to feel like the Michelin Man. My thighs grew thick, my abdomen grew squishy, and my cheeks looked as though I'd just had my wisdom teeth removed.

Day four brought with it a new IV location in my opposite hand. Chemo mornings moved like molasses. The tick tock of the clock and the rhythmic buzzing of the IV machine made time seem as though it was standing still. Often I tried to sleep the time away. But other times I looked longingly out the window at the summer sunshine and lush, green vegetation, before realizing I was too tired to enjoy it anyway.

When day five arrived, I was utterly exhausted. "Last one!" Mom stated the obvious in hopes to cheer me up. "Hang in there, Miss! Then you've got one treatment week under your belt. One down, two to go!"

"Yep," I forced a smile in return, trying not to shut down Mom's optimism. She was just trying to help. Luckily, another tasty surprise boosted my spirits. Fridays were free ice cream day, courtesy of Homestead Ice Cream.

Freedom from the Cancer Centre would taste so sweet. We planned to the lake

My Cosmic Hammer

right after chemo was complete for the duration of my recovery period. Never had I so desperately wanted to escape to the quiet solitude of the lake.

My Cosmic Hammer

right after chemo was complete for the duration of my recovery period. Never had I so desperately wanted to escape to the quiet solitude of the lake.

INJECTION REFLECTIONS

*"Fear sure feels real sometimes, but fear is just an emotion
rooted in a story that was contrived in the mind.
It's okay to feel through it, just don't live there."*
– *Kristin Pierce*

Giving myself injections was one of the lovely things I never thought I would have to do. I had no trouble with receiving needles, but giving one? To myself? That was a different story.

Chemotherapy doesn't differentiate between good cells and bad cells—it just kills everything in its path. Therefore, one of the side effects of chemo was that blood counts become depleted and bottom out while the body worked to produce new ones. For me, this would occur on day ten of my twenty-one day cycle. To help curb the effects, a small injection of GCSF, given daily for four days in a row, would help stimulate the body to encourage blood cells production. This little miracle drug cost a whopping $180 per vial—luckily, insurance covered the cost. Little did I know, this drug would become my lifeline after my body became beaten down by the effectiveness of chemotherapy.

After my first round of chemo, I was given four vials and two options: Since we would likely be at the lake in between chemo rounds, we could drive to the closest hospital to have the injection administered, or else I could administer it myself. I wasn't prepared for this, but the nurse gave me instructions anyway. Typically, this subcutaneous injection could go in the thigh or the abdomen. Since I was so thin, she suggested using my abdomen because there wasn't enough extra meat on my thighs. If I decided that I didn't want to do it myself, I could go see the nurse. It seemed like it wouldn't be a big deal...that was, until day eight of my first cycle rolled around and mom reminded me about my injections.

After procrastinating by busying myself with other tasks that were not a priority, like playing with Diesel, Mom reminded me again. Finally, I stood in the kitchen at the lake and pulled the white, pharmacy paper bag from the fridge. I opened it and pulled out a needle, a vial, and a sterilizing pad. More slowly and thoroughly than ever before, I washed my hands at the sink. Then, stalling, I slowly opened the sterilizing pad and cleaned the majority of my abdomen as I mentally and emotionally processed what I had to do. The cold sensation of the sterilization wipe sent shivers up my spine, activating my already triggered nervous system. Gently, I practiced pinching various areas of my stomach to find the best injection site, then cleaned the area again.

Mom could tell I was hesitating. "Do you need any help? We can go to the hospital if you'd rather have the nurse do the injection for you."

That's a 30-minute drive for a ten-second injection, I thought. *What a waste of gas. This isn't a big deal. I can handle it,* I told myself.

"No, I'm okay," I lied. "I'm just taking my time."

Finally, I grabbed the vial, poked the needle into it, and drew up the magic medicine that would help my blood cells get back on track. I pinched a fold of skin on my abdomen and brought the needle to my skin until I felt a poke, then pulled it back.

Panic swept through me.

I took a breath and tried again. And again. Each time, the sharp tip of the needle scared me more than the time before. Each time, I held my breath.

Ugh. I let out a huge exhale of frustration. I just couldn't get past that initial poke to push the needle into my skin.

Why is this so scary?

Countless needles had penetrated the surface of my skin in the past several weeks. I was no stranger to needles, and I had become perfectly comfortable with watching the nurses push needles through the barrier of my skin and into my veins. Why was this such a big deal for me now? Because pushing the needle into my own body was something I'd never imagined having to do.

After what felt like an eternity of failed attempts, giving up, then trying again, I knew I had to make this happen. I took a break to give myself an internal mental pep talk until I built up enough of a courage reserve and was ready to give it another go. I brought the needle to my skin, felt the poke, and held it in place as I took one more deep breath. I closed my eyes and recited, "I can do this" in my head, then pushed the needle past the threshold of my skin and past the point of no return.

I opened my eyes to see the tip of the needle had penetrated the fold of skin I had pinched between my fingers. A huge sigh of relief left my lungs. Slowly and steadily, I finished pushing the short needle all the way into my skin. Then, all that remained was pushing the medication in—that part was easy.

Tears filled my eyes as I could finally breathe again. My shoulders dropped down from my ears, back to their natural resting position as I released the emotional burden and pressure I had been anxiously holding in.

First one, down. The first one was always the hardest.

FEVER EMERGENCY

"Allow yourself to release the emotions
you have struggled all your life to contain."
– Ellen Bass

A s day ten of my first chemo cycle approached, I attempted to shove my ever-growing fear back down. I didn't know what to expect, but the idea of "my blood cell count bottoming out" was not something I looked forward to experiencing. The anticipation and apprehension rose to an all-time high and consumed my racing thoughts when I didn't have something to distract me from myself. I avoided my emotions and bottled everything inside my already overloaded body, making matters worse.

By day nine, my warrior mask started to slip. Fear had completely taken over and it was becoming obvious that my bodymind was struggling. My body temperature had been slowly, but steadily, on the rise and I felt outrageously tired with every fibre of my weary being. Something was happening inside my body, and it was definitely not good. With my mask slipping, it was becoming visible that I was not okay at all.

I went for a nap hoping that it would settle my mind while helping my body heal, but I woke up feeling worse. The internal alarms started ringing inside of me. It was time to stop trying to be a hero. I went upstairs and after a slow, laborious climb up the thirteen steps from the basement, I was out of breath and looked like hell. Diesel came over and licked my leg, but I didn't feel good enough to reciprocate the love. Mom could see it in my eyes as she monitored me like a hawk. She called my chemo nurse for advice and packed us up to head home to Rosetown to be closer to Saskatoon in case we had to rush to the hospital.

When we got to Rosetown, I laid on the couch at home feeling like absolute junk. My mouth tasted like metal, I was wildly uncomfortable, and I felt like I had been hit by a train. My eyes filled with tears as I wondered how in the world I'd gotten here. *Where did I go wrong? Why do I deserve this?*

The pity party train had arrived and that was totally okay. My emotions bubbled to the surface when I finally stopped trying to hold my superwoman mask on tight. Of course, I quickly blinked back the tears when anyone was around. I wished I didn't feel that way, but I didn't want to risk anyone thinking I was doubting if I could conquer this mountain.

That night, I was so utterly exhausted that Mom helped me get ready for bed. She was very persistent with me, regularly checking my temperature and keeping close supervision—like the most serious case of helicopter mom. She checked my temperature one last time before bed, then she looked me in the eyes and made me promise I would wake her up in the night if my temperature was close to thirty-eight degrees Celsius. I agreed, knowing full well that now was not the time to be a hero. It just wasn't. This was serious and she made damn sure that I understood.

When I woke up sweaty at 1:00 a.m., there was no doubt in my mind that I had to wake up my parents, but doing so made me feel like a helpless child. I wasn't great at asking for real, honest, vulnerable help, so I first went to the bathroom while I hesitated. Luckily, Mom heard me right away and quietly knocked on the bathroom door. When I opened the door, our eyes met with concern and she instantly touched the back of her hand to my forehead.

"You're burning up. We have to go," she said with a mixture of fear and determination in her eyes.

She woke Dad, quickly stuffed a few essentials in an overnight bag, and they helped me to the car. While on the way, Mom called the hospital to tell them we were en route, then texted Christina, my BodyTalk practitioner, to request an emergency session. I tried to rest in the car, but the adrenaline within the vehicle ran at an all-time high. Dad cruised past 130kph knowing full well the severity of the situation we were in. My knees ached, so I gently rubbed them as I tried to breathe, stay calm, and tap my cortices.

When we arrived, Dad slammed the vehicle into park in front of the Emergency Room and Mom ran in ahead of us. When the ER staff moved with lightning speed, I knew things were serious. They immediately got me a wheelchair, commanded me to sit down, then wheeled me straight into the first triage room next to the check-in desk—with real walls and a door!

By the time I got settled in the bed, a nurse had already drawn up my blood work, started an IV, and got antibiotics running immediately. The nurses reassured my parents they had done the right thing by bringing me in. We all sighed an exhale of relief to finally be receiving care in the hands of medical professionals, but the look on the faces of the staff members was anything but comforting. My mask of bravery was far too heavy to bear anymore. My body was weary, and my mind was overloaded. Since the antibiotics were now coursing through my veins, I finally gave myself permission to feel the fear that was also flowing through my body and mind.

Before long, I began to experience the god-awful pain of my blood cell count bottoming out on day ten of my chemotherapy cycle. Excruciating didn't even begin to describe the level of pain I felt that night.

It began as an achy sensation in my knees that gradually became more prominent. Then, my ankles started to ache too. It started to intensify slowly, but over time the dial felt as though it was cranked full throttle. Now, to set the stage, let me note that I have always had an extremely high pain tolerance. As an athlete, I learned to become very good at "sucking it up" with a "no pain, no gain" mentality and, as a result, I built a pain tolerance that made me believe I was tough as nails. Needless to say, I functioned on an "emotions equaled weakness" mindset, so even though the situation terrified me, I refused to let it show. Holding all of my emotions in just created an emotional pile up inside my body and mind, which added to the severity of my symptoms.

Did you know that can happen? Emotions and thoughts can exacerbate symptoms when stuffed back inside the body instead of letting them flow and release. I didn't know this then, but I sure found out the hard way.

Before I knew it, the pain became completely unbearable. I couldn't get comfortable because my legs hurt so much and holding them still was excruciating. In no time flat, I was writhing in pain in the hospital bed— thrashing around, turning from side to side, and moving my legs as if I was riding an invisible bicycle. My jaw was clenched in agony, and I clung to the bed rails as if my life depended on it. It resembled a scene from a horror movie, and I couldn't imagine how helpless it made my parents feel.

As the intensity of my pain increased, Mom went to tell a nurse. I had never before was pain so intense that I couldn't bear to hold in my emotions for another second longer. Tears began pouring out of my eyes like a faucet. I couldn't hold it together, and I wish I would have realized that I never really needed to.

Dad asked, with tear-filled eyes, to describe what the pain felt like. I could barely find the words to describe the bone-chilling pain that radiated through every cell of my body. The intensity was completely unfathomable and unlike anything I had ever experienced before. Then, finally, the description came to me, and I choked out the words, "It feels like someone is sawing through my knees."

It felt like an eternity of pain in Dante's Hell by the time a nurse finally came with an IV bag of pain killers. As the medication moved through my body, the first sign of relief gave me hope. My muscles relaxed as I took a deep breath in and let out a desperate sigh of relief. I wiped my wet, blotchy face and soon realized the depth of my own exhaustion. I was drained, in shock, and in shambles.

At 4:00 a.m., after the worst few hours of my life, exhaustion pulled me into sleep to the sound of beeping monitors. I was exhausted, but I was alive.

When I woke at 8:30 a.m., it felt as though sleep had held me in its embrace for only a few minutes. Exhaustion consumed me. My eyes felt like they had been sandblasted, and every inch of my body ached with soreness. I wasn't sure what to think, how to feel, or how to process what had happened the night before. I was just glad it was behind me.

When Dr. Giede came in to check on me, he explained that my white blood cell count had dropped down to 0.7, a number with extreme implications that I was glad I hadn't known about the night before. White blood cells help the body fight off infection, so when he told us the normal white blood cell count range is from 4.0 to 10.5, it meant that a count of 0.7 was dangerously low. Like, could-have-died low. Had my body been in contact with any kind of virus, bacteria, or any other pathogen, my immune system wouldn't have had a fighting chance. An ear infection could have killed me. *Whoa.*

I did not have the mental capacity to process that news. I felt traumatized and in shock from the events of the night before and knew I needed a BodyTalk session. As sleep pulled me back in, I let it.

Soon, I was transferred up to an isolated hospital room. Since my immune system was basically nonexistent, I had to be contained in a sterile environment to minimize my risk of exposure. Once I got settled, the feelings of frustration and doom towards being confined in the hospital yet again began to creep in. *Sweet, another five days in the hospital,* I thought, laced with sarcasm, as I rolled my eyes. My attitude only worsened when I realized I'd be in the hospital for another long weekend.

Visitation was limited as it was imperative that I was not exposed to any viruses or bacteria while my body worked over-time to recuperate. When anyone entered my hospital room, a blue mask covered their nose and mouth, while the scent of hand sanitizer wafted toward my sensitive nose as they rubbed their hands together.

The beautiful summer weather called to me, or at least it looked beautiful out from the view of the hospital room I felt trapped in. Obviously, my reasons for being there were far more serious than I wanted to admit but, at the same time, I just longed to be a normal twenty-one-year-old for a single long weekend that summer. Instead, I laid in isolation in a hospital bed while my blood count recovered. Impatience, frustration, and envy coursed through me when I thought of my friends off gallivanting at the lake, while I was stuck within the sterile confines of this hospital room. But, hey, I should have been more grateful. I could have died. My brush with death was far closer than I had ever realized. Maybe I didn't want to see that though, considering the stark reality of two more rounds of chemo ahead of me. That fever would only be the first gigantic obstacle—that thought in itself was beyond terrifying. It didn't feel like a great time to be wallowing in grief.

As I laid exhausted in the hospital bed that I was getting far too used to, I had to put my long, blonde hair into neatly woven braids to hide the fact that so much of it was falling out. I knew that it could be normal for people to experience hair loss after a major surgery. I wasn't exactly sure if it was the trauma or the anaesthesia that affected the body, but either way, I begged for that to be all that was happening.

On top of that, as if the hair wasn't embarrassing enough, fever blisters had begun to develop all over my face. Initially thinking they were acne, instead of understanding they were my body's normal reaction to the insane fever of the night before, I put some white acne cream on them in an awkward attempt to dry them up.

"Those are probably from your high fever the last night, not breakouts," Dr. Giede noted when he came to check on me.

"Oh," I said, embarrassed. I wanted to crawl into a hole and hide. Apparently, that was the one perk to being in isolation.

After spending a total of five days in the hospital, I was finally cleared for release. My in-patient tally had grown to nineteen days, plus five days of out-patient chemotherapy within seven weeks of summer. I was itching to run out of the hospital before I had to report back for my next round of chemo. Never had five days of freedom sounded so sweet.

MUSIC IS HEALING

"Music can heal the wounds that medicine cannot touch."
– Debasish Mridha

On the day I was being released from the hospital, the Saskatoon Exhibition was on. Mark had asked if I wanted to go see Nickelback play at the grandstands. He mentioned that he had already bought the tickets and was just trying to find someone to go with him. I knew that wasn't the whole truth. He knew how much I loved concerts and also saw how much I needed a getaway from my reality. I desperately wanted to go.

I love concerts with an absolute passion. There is just something about watching a musician in their element—bravely putting themselves out there to the world—that I wildly admire. Concerts inspire me, get me grooving, and truly make my heart feel happy.

"Can I go? Can I? Can I?" I, once again, asked my parents. If they were hesitant the time before, the resistance was ten-fold this time. If I was in their position, I don't think I would have let me go. But, that was beside the point. They could see the desperation in my eyes. Heck, I could hear it in my voice. *Please let me be normal for two hours.* Mom agreed on one condition: I had to take a blue hospital mask with me and wear it whenever I was in the thick of the crowds. I agreed, reluctantly, even though I didn't want to wear it at all. *How embarrassing,* I thought. Luckily the concert was outside, so the open air was a win.

*W*hat should I wear? I wondered.

Since my incision went down to my pubic bone and my scar still felt sensitive, the idea of wearing jeans worried me. I carefully put on a pair of jeans and looked in the mirror. The chemo swelling in my body had mostly dispersed, and I was back to skin and bones. My hair was thinning where it parted on the top of my head. Tears welled up in my eyes. I was overly aware of what was happening, but I was already too backlogged with emotional processing to call attention to it.

The voice in my head piped up for a pep talk: *Just make yourself feel pretty and go enjoy yourself. Set down your worries and act like a twenty-one-year-old for a couple of hours.*

Mom handed us masks as we headed out the door for the concert. *Perfect.*

When we got to the Exhibition, my cravings were on point: I wanted a Hawaiian Ice. We found the stand, and Mark insisted on buying it for me. He always did that—he got that from his mom. She was always adamant on paying for things. A twinge of guilt ran through my body and I noticed the reservations I felt internally—I didn't want him to get the wrong idea. I knew he just wanted to help, but I didn't want to blur the boundary lines of our friendship by accepting his generosity. In the end, I graciously accepted his generosity, knowing he needed to feel like he was helping me. And, he was, more than he or I probably ever realized in that moment. But it wasn't in the gifts or the outings. It was in his support; his treating me in the same, supportive way he always had; in the comfort and normalcy his friendship, sense of humour, and presence provided.

We headed to the grandstands and sat while I ate my treat—the Hawaiian Ice was as delicious as I expected. When the concert started, we sat and watched the opening band. At the intermission, I leaned over to Mark and said, "Let's go down to the floor."

"Are you sure?" he asked hesitantly.

"Yep! I want to see this up close! There's lots of space down there," I said with excitement illuminating my face. Like I said, concerts fire me up and light a spark in my soul. "Let's go!"

"Okay," he said, reluctantly. He wanted me to feel free tonight, but also felt responsible to keep me safe and make sure I didn't overdo it. I'm sure my mom's voice echoed in the back of his mind all night.

We made our way down to the grandstand stairs to the floor. It wasn't crowded like an indoor concert, so we kept our distance from others, but I was still hyper-aware of the people around me. Fear ran high in my mind. Anytime I heard a cough or a sneeze, I hot tailed it out of that person's vicinity. I knew enough to understand the severity of what my body was dealing with.

Nickelback came on stage and lit the place up. While we weren't that close to the stage, the pyrotechnics still lit up the night and warmed my skin. I could feel the bass rumbling through my chest while the music rattled my eardrums. I sang along at the top of my lungs and danced my heart out. It was the best therapy. I felt so free, so connected, and so inspired.

Cancer doesn't stand a chance.

My heart was happy to be out and be free, even if it was just for a few hours. But eventually, the concert had ended and my body had grown weary and was asking for gentleness. I knew it was time to listen to my body's cues and head home for the night. I was gassed. That was a lot of walking for a girl who had just been lying in a hospital bed for five days straight.

That night, I drifted off to sleep with ringing eardrums, a happy heart, and a perma-smile on my face. That was exactly what I needed.

IT ALL FALLS DOWN

"Rock bottom will teach you lessons that mountain tops never could."
– Unknown

I came into this world with an outrageously thick head of hair. I never fully appreciated that fact. Trained to want what we don't have, I coloured, changed, cut, and rejected my natural hair for most of my adolescent and adult life.

It is mind-blowing to consider how much power we give to our hair. It becomes an identity to many of us. It becomes a measure of time. It becomes a way we remember and hold onto our past. But we are so much more than our hair—*so much more*. Your hair is simply an expression of you. It is not who you are.

My naturally thick hair continued to disappear in the days following my release from the hospital. I kept it in braids to preserve as much of it as possible, for fear of what was coming around the next bend. Even so, when it came time for a shower, I felt blindsided by what was about to happen.

As I stood in the shower and attempted to shampoo my hair, I began to feel the thickness of my hair moving away from my scalp. I removed my head from the stream of water, and sheer panic took over as I was hit with the realization of what was happening.

Oh, my God!

The weight of the water falling from the shower head was enough to detach much of it from my scalp. Quickly, I did my best to get the shampoo out of my hair, while desperately trying to support the strands as I rinsed it. I could already feel the tangled mess that I would have to attempt to get a brush through, so conditioner was a must. Never in my life had I been so eerily aware of the weight of the water.

As I turned off the shower and delicately squeezed the water from my hair, I looked down to find a pile of hair in the bottom of the tub. I closed my eyes and begged, "Please, no." Terrified of the reality that was about to confront me, I carefully climbed out of the shower to see a broken body staring back at me in the mirror. My eyes rose from the sight of my healing scar across my abdomen to the matted mess above my head. The reflection staring back at me seemed so foreign. I felt like a stranger in my own body, and my heart shattered into a million pieces.

Why? I asked myself. *Why can't I catch a break?*

I felt a mixture of fear and desperation move through my body, as I tried to work my way through the rat's nest with a brush. After three separate brushing sessions, it became very evident there was way too much hair coming out of my head. *No. Please, no.* I repeated as I inspected the growing bald spot that appeared where I parted my hair in the middle. *Not this too.*

By the time I completed brushing my hair, a huge hairball consumed the entirety of the bathroom sink. I picked it up with two hands and took it to the living room to show my parents. Disgusted and desperate, I said, "Look how much hair came out of my head."

Mom and Dad exchanged a panicked glance, hoping that I didn't need to add "losing my hair" to the list of devastation being done to my already tired heart. Mom made an emergency hair appointment with our hair stylist, Starla. Because my hair was so long, heavy, and thick, we figured it might be worth chopping some of the weight off, in hopes that it wouldn't all fall out. Denial or wishful thinking?

As I sat down in the Starla's chair at her home salon, the lump in my throat had reached an all-time high. Already fearing the inevitable that I had been trying so hard to avoid, she broke the sad news. As she touched a small section and ran her fingers through it, out came half of the hair she'd been holding. "I'm barely touching it and almost all of it is coming out. The follicle isn't holding onto the root anymore. I'm really sorry, but it's going to fall out."

My eyes welled with tears, my jaw clenched, and my throat tightened. I felt like I'd been pulled underwater all over again. My mind raced as my heart shattered on the floor. I could barely breathe.

This can't be happening. Dr. Giede said I wasn't going to lose my hair. Why is it falling out?! This isn't supposed to happen. No. Please no. I felt angry, broken, and betrayed. I wasn't prepared for this.

Mom and Starla talked through our options, although I could barely hear the conversation over the screaming voices inside my mind.

"Do you want me to buzz it?" Starla asked.

I couldn't hide the tears anymore. This was way too much for my heart to handle. "No. I'm not ready for this, yet," I finally squeaked. I felt like I was suffocating and gasping for air.

"Okay, well how about we chop it shorter for you so it's easier to manage until you're ready."

Thankful that she'd taken the reins and made a suggestion, I quickly nodded, unable to form a sentence. It was all happening too fast. I needed some time to process that my fourteen inches of luscious, thick locks were no longer being held by my scalp. *How is this even happening?* I was holding out for a miracle. I wasn't ready to let go of what my hair represented. Not yet, anyway. I needed some time to let it all sink in.

Starla told us about wig shops in Saskatoon, along with tips to manage my hair until then, since my head seemed to be shedding like a Husky in the spring. "Put a bandana around your head before you go to sleep. That way, you won't have piles of hair all over your bed in the morning."

Mom quickly got on the phone to one of the wig shops in Saskatoon as Starla's shears chopped my hair into a bob. "We have to leave right away, or we won't make it before they close," Mom noted. When Starla finished up, we exchanged hugs and thanked her, then headed to the car. I felt completely devastated as we raced the clock to make it to the city before closing time. We were pushing it for time but managed to arrive five minutes before closing. Luckily, the owner graciously kept the store open longer for us, as I was sure she was no stranger to the devastating feeling of losing one's hair.

She mentioned that she had alopecia and had long since been a regular wig wearer. She told us about the variety of wigs she owned and how it had become fun to play around with her hairstyle with more freedom than she would have ever allowed herself before. Wow, that's brave, I thought to myself. For a moment, this brief interaction opened my panicked mind, ever so slightly, to the idea that losing my hair didn't have to be the worst experience in the world. I wasn't ready to fully absorb that, but it seemed to have been noted and filed in my subconscious to revisit at a later date.

Have you ever been in a wig shop? There are so many options, which is super fun when you're just looking for a wig *for fun*, but when you are there because you're going to be bald, it's mostly just overwhelming. There were so many lengths, colours, and styles. Some were way too "old lady-like", others just not my style. After keeping the store open for an extra twenty minutes, I knew this was a big decision that I was far too emotional to make. Plus, the wigs were expensive—we were talking upwards of $400-800 or more. As Mom asked about insurance coverage, I knew I was too emotionally volatile to make a big decision like this. We thanked her and mentioned we'd be back the next day.

I had to endure an entire evening of devastating hair-loss reality before I could get a wig to cover up my pain. *Dammit.*

This all may sound incredibly vain. It's only hair—what's the big deal, right? "It'll grow back," they said. "You are beautiful no matter what," they stated. But it was a really big deal to me. For our entire lives, we are conditioned by magazines, commercials, movies, TV, and celebrities that show us a definition of beauty. Where does a bald, swollen, pasty cancer patient fit into that mold? To me, she didn't.

That night, I was a big jerk. I was so rude to my mom. Since she was always around, she became my punching bag, which was wildly unfair. I snapped at the drop of a hat and was triggered by anything and everything that happened around me. I felt like the wind had been sucked from my lungs as I suffocated and gasped for a breath of air that never came. Terrified, I was in panic mode without a shred of patience left to my name. I was hurting in a way I had never known before. This didn't even compare to finding out I had cancer, because I really didn't see this one coming.

Until this point, even though I was sick, I still looked relatively like myself. So, although there was a war taking place inside my body, it wasn't very obvious to a random stranger that there was anything wrong with me. Losing my hair meant I would look like a cancer patient. Losing my hair would make all of this just way too real.

WHY? What did I do to deserve this? Please, someone, just make it all stop. My stomach was in knots. I was fuming with anger. It felt like an elephant was sitting on my chest. *Is it going to grow back? What the hell am I going to do? I hate this.* I wanted to scream, but instead I held it all in and spewed at my mom. My poor mom.

After about the thirtieth rude comment I'd made to my mom that night, she'd finally had enough. She snapped back and put me in my place. Enraged, I stormed off to my room. I knew I was not being kind, but every fibre of my heart had shattered, and I ached with grief. The anger was a front, but it was all I could muster. I had never felt so broken before, so helpless.

Later, Mom knocked on my bedroom door.

"What?" I asked in a snotty voice.

She opened the door. "I know you're upset, but you can't keep holding it all inside and taking it out on me. You've got to find a way to let it out. Here," she said as she handed me paper and a pen. "Write a letter. Write me a letter. Tell me how you're feeling if you want to. I don't care what you do, but you've got to get it out."

At first, I was just pissed off that she had the nerve to tell me what to do. *As if you know how I'm feeling right now,* I thought. My blood boiled. *As if you have any idea what I am going through!*

After my anger cooled down, I grabbed the paper and thought about what I wanted to write. Instantly, everything that I'd been holding inside for the past six weeks began pouring out of my eyes like an unstoppable waterfall. A steady stream of tears raced down my cheeks, landing on the bed and soaking the sheets I sat on. I soaked and snotted my way through a mountain of Kleenex as words poured out onto the paper and I got a glimpse inside my broken heart.

I felt devastated. My whole world was crumbling all around me. The ground was shaking beneath my trembling legs, and it was just too much to bear. I felt as if I was breaking and I couldn't hold myself together anymore. The last thing I wanted was to look like a cancer patient. Now, here I was about to officially become part of the chemo club. I was terrified.

I took the letter to Mom, who was in her room getting ready for bed. I handed her the letter, and with tears in my eyes and possibly the blotchiest red face known to man, I apologized for being so awful. She hugged me and we cried together.

That night, I slept with a bandana on my head. As soon as I woke up in the morning, I took the bandana off to inspect it. *Did I get my miracle?* I begged. I squeezed my eyes shut in an attempt to will a new reality into existence. Upon opening my eyes, I saw the bandana was covered in hair—absolutely covered. *Damn.*

I took the bandana to show Mom. I felt sheepish after being such a jerk to her the night before when she was doing absolutely everything in her power to ease my pain and soften the blow of this new devastation.

"What do you think?" Mom asked, carefully. "Do you want to go see Pam today?"

Pam was my mom's cousin and a hairdresser in Saskatoon. Knowing she worked on Saturdays meant that she could hopefully help us out. I nodded my head. The last thing either of us needed was for Mom to shave my head, given the volatile emotional state I was in. She called ahead as I awkwardly fumbled around the house "getting ready" for the most heartbreaking moment of my life. *What should I wear?* Nothing could soften the blow of the harsh reality that was about to hit me. A cloak of invisibility would have been the only thing to help me feel better.

We packed up and headed to Pam's salon. I attempted to distract myself with a magazine while we waited. It didn't help much as most options were hair magazines. But as much as I didn't want to accept my new reality, it was helpful to check out the hairstyles that might interest me in a wig. I struggled to stay positive while Mom tried to cheer me up. Yet, nothing could distract me from the awful sinking feeling that sat in the pit of my stomach. Impending baldness would soon occupy my scalp where my luscious locks once securely sat.

This wasn't supposed to happen, echoed in my mind.

Pam called me over and tried to keep things light, giving complements and attempting to lighten the heavy emotional load that I carried on my shoulders. While she prepared and chatted with Mom, I focused on my breath as I stared into the eyes of my reflection and blinked back tears. This heartbreaking moment continually etched in my mind, moment by moment.

The buzz of the hair clippers made me jump and sent chills up my spine. *Oh, my God. This is it.*

"Are you ready?" she asked sweetly.

God no. How can I be ready for this? I took a deep inhale and let out a heavy sigh.

"Yep," I lied.

Pam pressed the clippers gently to the side of my head near my right temple, then made a clean sweep backwards above my ear. The hair fell down my right shoulder and onto the floor. I stared straight ahead at my teary reflection in the mirror, already pasty and pale after just one round of chemo.

"The first one is always the hardest," she said.

As she continued, passing the clippers over my scalp from front to back, one strip at a time, the reality and severity of my health situation hit me with an indescribable velocity.

I can't hide it anymore. I can't pretend I'm okay. I definitely wasn't okay.

The sound of the clippers and my bald and shattered reflection were forever etched into my memory. As much as it broke me to watch this all unfold, I felt the tiniest glimpse of relief wash over me. It was almost over. With each pass, a feeling of grief danced with a twinge of relief as my hair (and my confidence) fell to the floor.

I walked out of the hair salon feeling a mixture of heartbreak and relief. With each inhale, it felt as though I was struggling to inhale a tropical humid air. My chest felt tight and my throat was barely able to squeak out any words. But my exhales poured out of me like waves crashing on the shore. It had been the heaviest and most emotional day of my entire life.

If this didn't break me, nothing could.

THE HAIR WE WEAR

"**D**o you want to go get a wig, Miss?" Mom asked as we made our way from Pam's salon to the car.

I nodded as I blinked back the tears that threatened to surface. My throat was so tight it felt like I was choking.

"Deep breaths, Miss," Mom reminded me. I nodded again. We drove to the wig shop, and I had no words for what I was feeling. I had some major processing to do. Thankfully, Mom booked me a BodyTalk session while I was in the salon.

As we entered the wig shop, I told Mom that I wanted to find something that was similar to the style and colour of my hair before it all fell out. I wasn't emotionally prepared to let go of me old identity yet. I'd endured enough unexpected change and I desperately wanted to feel steady ground under my feet—I wanted to feel like myself, even though I really didn't know what that meant anymore.

It took a few attempts, but after trying on a few wigs, I found one that was a close enough match. I was desperate to cover up my vulnerability.

"Your hairdresser can cut it so it suits your style," the saleswoman added. And after learning basic wig techniques of how to place it on my head and how to care for it, we decided to escape to the lake for the rest of the weekend. I would worry about getting it styled later.

I sighed with relief as my body melted into the seat for a car nap.

My Cosmic Hammer

That night, I got dolled up with my new wig and went to a rodeo dance with some friends. Awkward, uncomfortable, and nervous didn't even begin to describe my feelings as I stood on the cement floor of the arena, making small talk with friends. It felt like I was hiding something, and that's probably because I was. In many ways, I felt like an imposter in my own life. When I was feeling self-conscious to begin with, it felt like everyone was staring at me with an enormous amount of judgement. If I hadn't just lost all of my hair that same day, maybe I wouldn't have felt so insecure, but the fearmongering voice inside my mind was getting the better of me.

Is my wig on crooked? Does it look fake? Can they tell it's not real? Why is everyone staring at me?

Mid-way through my inner monologue of self-doubt, my buddy, Carter, came up to me. "KP!" he said as he hugged me tight. "I like your hair," he said, putting his hands on my head. My heart skipped a beat.

Oh my god, he's touching my wig! I thought wide-eyed and panicked.

"Your hair looks great!" he said, still touching it.

I didn't like hiding. My nerves couldn't handle it and my stomach was in knots. Not that it was anyone else's business but, clearly, I needed to own my situation instead of hiding it. So, I decided to be honest.

"Oh, thank you," I replied, smiling. "It's a wig."

His face turned white and his jaw dropped open. "Shit, KP! I'm so sorry." He clutched his chest. "It looks so real. I had no idea." He looked like a deer in the headlights until I smiled and started laughing.

"Doesn't it!?" I said laughing. "That's okay. Don't even worry about it."

"Whoa, so you lost your hair?" he asked, attempting to make sense of the news. "I thought you said it wasn't supposed to fall out."

"I was told it wasn't supposed to," I replied. "But so much was falling out, so we buzzed it off this morning and just got this wig this afternoon."

"Oh, I'm so sorry," Carter said, still touching his chest as he let out a big sigh.

"It's okay," I smiled and said as I opened my arms to give him a hug. "Honestly, it really is."

Later, when I was talking with some girlfriends, another friend, Boo, came up and gave me a big hug. "I thought someone said that you lost your hair?" he said, reaching for my head.

Oh no. Not again.

"I did," I confirmed, as I backed away from his grasp.

"Really?" he asked, looking visibly confused. "So, that's a wig?" I smiled as he connected the dots. "Wow. It looks good," he nodded.

"You're so brave," one of my girlfriends said.

"You look great," said another as she gently petted the side of my wig. "It honestly looks so real. I would have never known if you didn't say anything."

While in my mind, I had a refuting comment for each of their remarks, the tension in my body began to subtly melt as the truth came out and no longer had to hold it inside. There was no space for that anyway. My body was at capacity for mental, emotional, and physical processing. Hiding my wig required way more energy than it did to be honest about it. And honesty created an incredible web of support from even the mostly unlikely of places. What a lesson that was. That night began to put things in perspective, which was the swift kick in the ass that I so desperately needed.

It was time to be grateful that I was alive and well enough to even have the minuscule concerns of a wig cramping a Saturday night with my friends.

As I looked out the window, remembering back to that night, I saw a bright purple colour out of the corner of my eye. I turned to see my daughter, Aspen, stepping into my high heels. She wore an elegant princess dress, white gloves, a pearl necklace, and a purple wig.

"Ooooh, don't you look fancy, girlfriend!"

"Why, thank you," she replied, clomping around the basement. "Where did you get this fancy hair from, Mom?"

"That was from my stagette, girly."

She stopped in her tracks and looked at me with wide eyes as she crinkled her nose. "What's a stagette?"

"It's a party that girls have with their girlfriends before one of them gets married. Boys have them too, except they're called stags for boys," I explained.

She looked at me puzzled.

"That's the Saskatchewan lingo, anyways. Other places call them bachelor and bachelorette parties," I finished.

"That's weird," and she carried on with her clomping. Then she paused again. "So, did you wear this to your party?" She said pointing to her head.

"Yep!" I smiled. "I had a wig party! It was so fun. There were so many different colours of wigs."

"What colour did Meemee wear?" Aspen asked, referring to my mom.

"Meemee wore a green one; Auntie Channy wore a long, fuscia one; and Auntie Kate's was a curly, blonde wig. Let's go see if we can find a picture of it," I said, and she clomped behind me down the hallway towards our photo album collection.

BALD DOESN'T FEEL BEAUTIFUL

"Don't believe everything you think."
– Unknown

When I returned to the Cancer Centre for my second round of chemo, I looked the part of a cancer patient, and I hated that truth with every fibre of my being. I felt devastated and destroyed, pasty white and embarrassed. I had tried to convince myself that I didn't belong there, but it had become blatantly obvious that I now fit right in with the crowd. The label I had tried to avoid since the day I'd walked in was "cancer patient". Just like that, my confidence drained out of me like the pigmentation in my skin.

You know those well-meaning comments that people say to help you feel better? Well, they didn't help me feel better—at all.

"You look great!"

"You're so beautiful—it doesn't even matter if you have hair."

"She's a natural beauty," Mom would add.

"You have such a nice-shaped head."

"Not everyone can pull that look off, but you sure can."

"You're beautiful."

"Oh, thanks," I'd respond with a lacklustre expression. Every uninvited reaction was the last thing I wanted to hear. Instead, the comments were a constant reminder of how obvious it was that I was sick. I couldn't hide it anymore. I felt so raw and vulnerable that I wanted to crawl into a hole and hibernate into eternity.

But this was exactly how it needed to unfold for me. There was no doubt in my mind that this was the pivotal launch pad on my journey to healing—letting go of who I thought I was, who I thought I had to be, and all the other stories I had been telling myself for far too long. Without chemotherapy and losing my hair, I wouldn't have had to question who I really was. It took losing so much of who I thought I was physically to stop me in my tracks. What a powerful gift it was, even though I didn't see it that way at the time.

On day two of that round of chemo, and as per Mom's suggestion, Dad and I went out to search for some hats to cover my bald head on the days I wouldn't want to wear my wig. At that point, Mom and I both needed a break from each other, and I knew she was also trying to get Dad more involved so he could take part in what we had been going through.

As Dad and I walked around the mall, he got a front row seat to the awkward looks, the not-so-nonchalant glances, and the outright stares in my direction from passersby. At first, I tried to pretend I didn't notice, but it was no use. We were both blatantly aware of my tension as I struggled to keep my chin up. Seeing my emotional pain was tough on him and hit him harder than ever before. Dad desperately wanted to ease my discomfort. Already devastated, he bore witness to my broken heart as we wove in and out of stores on the lookout for hats to mask my frightening reality. In the end, we found three styles of hats that covered my entire head and slightly eased the self-consciousness I felt without my hair. The hats gave me permission to not have to pretend to be my old self by wearing my wig all the time. But, more importantly, we found comfort, support, and connection in each other's presence and from experiencing a healing moment together, just the two of us.

The next day, as Dr. Giede entered the exam room for my mid-chemo round check-up, he looked at me with surprise and stopped in his tracks. "Oh..." he paused. "Your hair fell out."

Is that a question or a statement, I wondered? I couldn't tell if he was shocked because he cared or if he didn't think it was a big deal. He dealt with cancer patients all the time. Life over hair was the obvious priority.

"Um...yep," I replied with the sarcastic tone of an unimpressed teenager. What I really wanted to say was, "No shit, Sherlock!" or "Thanks, Captain Obvious!" But, I refrained. I was already sick of the lack-of-hair comments and it seemed they were just getting started.

He'd told me my hair wouldn't fall out, and I had believed him. I felt angry and naïve, betrayed and blindsided. I wished, so badly, that he would have just told me that my hair would fall out. At least then I would have had time to mentally and emotionally prepare myself for the devastation. I was fuming on the inside with a hurting heart to match, but I did my best to hide it.

"I really wasn't expecting that to happen," he said apologetically.

In that moment, I think he saw the profound hurt in my eyes. I softened a little, as it became obvious that he truly wasn't expecting that to happen. So often we expect doctors to know everything. We expect them to have all the answers and we take every word they say as gospel. But doctors are human too. Dr. Giede couldn't have seen into the future to know how my body would react to the chemicals being pumped into it. So, I couldn't blame him for not being able to accurately predict how my body would respond to chemotherapy.

My emotions moved to the surface as I finally put down my armour. That was the first time Dr. Giede saw me without my facade of strength walled up around me.

My Cosmic Hammer

I was told that I wouldn't lose my hair. So why did it fall out?

My doctor said he was 90% sure that chemo wouldn't affect my hair. But if I'd whole-heartedly believed him in the first place, then I wouldn't have had to ask for a percentage. I was already in doubt because I was so scared of "looking" like a cancer patient.

It was my biggest fear. "Please don't make my hair fall out" was the phrase that ran on repeat through my mind. I tried to stuff it down, ignore it, and pretend it wasn't happening.

There were many layers underneath this attachment to my physical appearance. To me, looking sick, again, meant weakness. It meant that everyone would know that my "strength" was a facade. Losing my hair made it all too real. Without hair, I could no longer hide what I was going through. Without hair, I had to face my reality. I didn't want to go there, but avoidance is never a healthy coping mechanism.

The only way I could have shifted my experience is if I had dived in to investigate, unravel, and dismantle the fear. Not only did I not know how to do that at the time, but I was also in intense survival mode. I was emotionally overloaded with little willingness to let my emotions surface. Luckily, my BodyTalk practitioner had helped me gently look at the fears, beliefs, and emotions I was trying so badly to push down. Yet, it still wasn't enough. It couldn't have gone any other way. And as much as I didn't realize it at the time, I needed this part the most.

Losing my hair was more traumatizing than being told I had cancer. And it needed to be. My hair was my protection. It helped me feel "normal" and "healthy" in a room full of bald cancer patients.

We have been conditioned to view cancer as a death sentence. Without hair, I didn't just look sick, I looked like a cancer patient, which I was desperately attempting to avoid. Even the most random stranger could see I was "sick". Looking sick meant that I could no longer hold up the mask of strength that I was so desperately trying to hide behind. People stared at me in the grocery store. The confidence-boosting comments from friends and family disappeared, along with my confidence. I could no longer pretend that everything was okay, when it so obviously wasn't. I was anything but okay. It was terrifying to admit that pretending to be strong all the time was a heavy burden to carry. Without hair, I felt bare, exposed, and raw. I can now see that is exactly how I needed to feel.

Losing my hair was the most transformational part of my journey. I needed to have everything stripped away so I could discover who I really was under all of the bullshit beliefs I thought I had to live up to all the time. The hiding was over. The masks had been ripped from my face. I was bare, bald, and more vulnerable than I had ever been in my life. Losing my hair shattered my heart and everything I once thought defined me. And in falling apart, came a wonderful opportunity to rebuild from scratch. I had to find myself by looking deeper than my appearance that I'd hid behind for so long. Instead, I had to find my heart, dive into my soul, and realize that my physical appearance had very little to do with who I truly was on the inside.

The blessing in disguise was that I got to start over. I got to redefine myself in so many ways I had never considered before. Being forced to let go of who I had always been gave room to create the space needed to discover who I really was. Over time, I found the courage to play, test, and do new things with my hair that I had been too chicken to try otherwise because I was so attached to the idea that my hair defined me. Along the way, I found the courage to try things outside of my designated "who I am" box, because that box was a big crock of crap anyway. I stopped taking life so seriously, and it was wildly freeing to blow the rules, expectations, and ideals I had built for myself right out of the water.

CORN POPS & MONSTER COOKIES

"Your body is always talking to you,
if you'd only slow down, get quiet, and listen."
– Kristin Pierce

With a second round of chemotherapy sloshing around in my body, I figured the least I could do was honour my body's requests and do my best to support it in healing—which was a huge light bulb moment for me. What I had learned as an athlete, which was further ingrained as a sports medicine student, was how to use my mind to tell my body what it needed. Through strict, disciplined routines, workout programs, and rigid meal plans, I learned that science knew what my body needed better than my body did. And, maybe that's true in some respects. But what if it's not?

Being on chemotherapy finally forced me to listen to my body. I know, it's ironic that I needed to have chemicals pumped into my body in order to learn about my body's wisdom, but I learned the hard way to sleep when I was tired, to sit down when I was running out of steam, and to ask for help when I needed it. So, when chemo cravings showed up, my BodyTalk practitioner suggested honouring my body's requests. Whoa.

And guess what? When I gave my body what it was asking for, I didn't feel nauseous. But when I forced myself to go against my body's wishes, I felt awful. Through much trial and error, I began to learn intuitive eating methods, without even realizing it.

Honouring my cravings became a fun adventure that brought a light feeling of playfulness and joy to a heavy experience. What does my body want today? I'd wonder upon waking in the morning. After years of telling myself what I had to eat and when, and then judging myself if I ate something I shouldn't, I was finally learning to let my body lead—and it felt so freeing.

"I want Corn Pops," I stated one morning, almost laughing.

"Really?" Mom asked, surprised with her eyebrows raised. I had become such a health nut after being immersed in sport, sports medicine, and nutrition classes that she was surprised to hear my request for sugary cereal.

"Yep," I laughed. "I don't even remember the last time I had Corn Pops. Maybe then years ago, but that's what my body wants," I said proudly.

"Okay," Mom shrugged. "When do you need them?"

"Right now," I laughed. "I need them now. These cravings are intense."

"No kidding. Okay, well let's get in the car then," Mom said, still smiling in disbelief.

"Oh, and monster cookies. I want to make monster cookies too," I added. It was 10:00 a.m.

"Monster cookies it is," Mom declared, and we were on the way.

We drove fifteen minutes to the closest store. Upon arrival, I wandered down the aisles, selecting the most random assortment of items my body requested. This was the first time, likely since childhood, that I was learning to listen to my body without judgement. I was simply honouring its requests—even if it wanted something not deemed as "healthy" for me.

I busted open the Corn Pops box the moment we loaded into the car. I couldn't wait another fifteen minutes. I munched on them until we got home, where I fixed myself a bowl of Corn Pops and milk. Shortly after, I began prepping the cookie dough for monster cookies. However, my stamina was so low from the chemo that my arms quickly grew tired. It was hard enough measuring ingredients, and in less than twenty second of mixing the dough, my arms burned with fatigue. I couldn't do it. Luckily, Dad had just arrived and was game to take over and finish the job.

My Cosmic Hammer

I can't even stir cookie dough for twenty seconds?! I thought as I went to rest on the couch. Admittedly, that took a bit of wind out of my sails. I took a deep breath and focused back on setting down my old expectations for myself as I waited for the cookies to be done.

I wasn't able to strong arm my way through this experience, which was how I'd always tackled my problems before. Now, I was being forced to learn how to listen to my body. When I was tired, I had to learn to go to bed. When my sense of smell was triggered, I had to learn to relocate before disgust turned into nausea. I learned the hard way when I overdid it. When I had a craving, I began to listen and honour my body's requests without judgement. So why not for this too? It was time to learn how to be gentle with myself. I finally gave myself permission to listen to my body and provide what it wanted without judgement. That felt pretty freeing.

FRIENDS FOR KEEPS

"Your heart and my heart are very old friends."
– Winnie the Pooh

One day, Mom mentioned that Lindsey's mom had called to check in on us. Remember the girl who quit her job when she couldn't get time off to come visit me in the hospital? That was Lindsey! She had been struggling with the news of me being sick and wanted to come for a visit. We had plans to go to the lake after my second round of chemo, and Mom and I both agreed that it would be nice to have some company, as long as I promised to not overdo it. Of course. I promised and was eager to have a visitor to look forward to, so Lindsey drove the five-hour trip for the second time that summer.

We had a nice, relaxing few days together which consisted of mainly of couch time, sun-bathing, reminiscing, gentle walks, girl talks, loads of snacks, playing with Diesel, laughter, and lots of movies. While I was worried that Lindsey would be bored, she was very caring, helpful, and patient with me, and that was exactly what I needed. Her presence had helped me open up and let my protective guard down. Our time together filled my heart and made my cheeks hurt from laughter.

Linds also made for a nice, and very necessary, buffer between Mom and me. The excessive amount of time Mom and I had spent together was starting to wear on both of us. My patience with her grew very thin at times. Since I had gotten used to living on my own for the past three years of college, having a helicopter Mom constantly overseeing my every move got old pretty quick. While it was necessary given the circumstances, I was very grateful to have Lindsey around for a few days to give Mom a break from my awful attitude. I knew I was being terrible, but I just couldn't seem to control myself. My emotional capacity was beyond full, and Mom unfortunately received the brunt of my emotional floods.

One evening, Mark, Lindsey, and I went to meet our friend, Colette, at the drive-in movie theatre, which was literally just a giant movie screen in the middle of a field. The movie didn't matter a smidge compared to how it felt to share the fun and laughter with my friends that night. We took some serious trips down memory lane as we cracked jokes and laughed until our cheeks hurt. The laughter was so good for the soul.

When it was time for Lindsey to return home, neither of us were ready for our time together to come to an end. So, she asked if I wanted to go back with her to Edmonton for a couple of days. When we asked Mom, I could tell the wheels were turning right away. Again, I knew she could see the desperation in my eyes. How can we make this work? I could see her thinking.

"Let me make a few phone calls first, then we can figure this out."

She didn't want to be too far away from me and that was understandable. Since Mom was always fourteen steps ahead of everyone else, she first called Lindsey's mom to discuss logistics, then called friends of hers in the Edmonton area to see if they were around. After that, she called the Cancer Centre to confirm it would be okay for me to travel out of province, along with our insurance provider to confirm that I would be able to receive out of province treatment or medication care if necessary. When dealing with something as serious as chemotherapy, I was glad that Mom was doing all the overthinking for me. I didn't have it in me to maintain that level of mental stamina.

"I talked to Lindsey's mom. You guys can head there tomorrow, and I'll follow you up the next day. I'll stay with Carrie and Jamie and then can bring you home."

Perfect, I thought. "Thanks, Mom!" I said excitedly as I hugged her tight. What I really meant was, "Thanks for not saying no. Thanks for helping me have somewhat of a normal existence."

The next day, Linds and I hit the highway in her white Eclipse. She drove as I rocked the role of CD jockey, curating the perfect composition of songs to sing at the top of our lungs. Our rap duets were on point after years of cruising around our small town, pumping the music, and nailing the lyrics. We laughed and reminisced, yet again, until our faces hurt. Whenever we were together, it was always a guaranteed good time.

When we finally arrived in Edmonton, I was wiped. Even after having a nap in the car, my stamina just wasn't anywhere close to what I had been used to all my life. While I knew Linds didn't care one bit, I felt guilty and lame for being such a drag. I wanted to have fun, but my body was working so hard under the surface of my skin that it just wasn't in me to even be the life of a retirement party.

I tried my best to keep up and hide my exhaustion as we went to tour her parents' new house they were building, then hung out in their fancy camping trailer for a while, but it was no use. It was written all over my face.

"Are you feeling okay?" Linds asked, looking empathetic and mildly concerned.

"Yeah, I'm okay. I'm just feeling really tired," I replied.

"You are looking pale," Linds added.

"Oh, that's just my wonderful colour from the chemo," I joked as I cracked a tired, half-smile. But I wasn't fooling anyone. The fatigue was written all over my face.

"You had better get Kristin to your place and just lay low for the night," Lindsey's mom suggested.

As we got back in the car, the sunset faded to darkness and fear began to set roots in my mind. I didn't realize how uncomfortable I would feel about not having my Mom around. For the entirety of the summer to date, she had always been close-by. Until now, I hadn't realized the sheer amount of comfort that her presence provided.

Exhausted, I got into my pyjamas and laid on the couch to watch a movie. I felt so far beyond fatigued that no words could even describe the feeling in my body. My mind had filled up with fear and my knees started to ache.

My Cosmic Hammer

Were you ever so tired that you didn't even want to get up to go to the bathroom? There were times when I felt sunken into the couch as if it was quicksand pulling me in. Chemo exhaustion was next level and unlike anything I had ever experienced before.

Linds looked at me, concerned. "Do you want to go to bed?" she asked.

"Yeah, I probably should," I replied with glassy eyes. Fear had filled my emotional reserves to the top of the spillway and I was teetering on the edge of just barely being able to hold myself together.

Though every fibre of my being was thoroughly exhausted, I couldn't manage to sleep. My mind began to race as the aching in my knees continued to grow. Shit, it's day nine. Why didn't I think of this before? What am I doing? Why did I think it was okay to come to Edmonton now? I shouldn't have come all this way. My blood cells are bottoming out. What if I need to go to the hospital?

I didn't want to be putting all of that responsibility on Lindsey, though I'm sure she was already feeling it. Fear was rampantly spreading through my body and mind, and as I worked myself up into a complete lather, my ankles joined the aching party.

Linds and I shared a bed, so I didn't want to disturb her by moving too much. Oh, how my legs ached though. I couldn't get comfortable no matter what I tried. It's no wonder I couldn't. The honest truth was that I was wildly uncomfortable being away from my mom and it was showing up in my body.

All my life, I believed it was important to be considerate. I didn't want to disturb anyone when others were sleeping, I patiently waited my turn, I didn't budge in line, and I followed the rules. Not only that, but I was always very independent with an I-can-handle-it-by-myself type of attitude, so it took a lot for me to ask for help. But how long would I suck it up?

I watched the minutes pass on the digital clock: 2:04 a.m., 2:08 a.m., 2:11 a.m.; eventually, 3:00 a.m. rolled as slow as molasses into 4:00 a.m. Just as I was about to drift into sleep, my aching joints and panicked mind jolted me awake.

Do I need to go to the hospital? Should I call Mom? Am I overreacting? What should I do?

195

In that moment, I needed to work the situation out on my own. Waking anyone up would have just added to my fear, and I couldn't handle any more than the amount I already carried. Eventually, I got up to check my temperature and settled in on the living room couch. As tears finally slid down my cheeks after 5:00 a.m., I drifted off to sleep as the morning sun peeked through the curtains and sent streaks of light across the room.

I WANT MY MOM

"Fear makes the wolf bigger than he is."
– German Proverb

"**H**ow did you sleep?" Linds asked.

"I'm not sure if I did," I replied, feeling bagged. "My knees are getting achy."

My fear had grown and it felt as though I couldn't contain it anymore. It must have been written all over my face. The memory of my last round of chemo was too fresh in my mind.

What if I get another fever? What if this pain means that my blood cells are bottoming out again?

The last thing I wanted to do was to put the responsibility of my health and my life on Lindsey. We were only twenty-one. I had been living this nightmare and I didn't even want to have to deal with this, so I couldn't imagine how hard it was on her. I needed my Mom.

"What do you want to do today?" Linds asked.

"I think I need to go meet up with my mom," I said, reluctantly. My throat was tight, and I blinked back tears. I didn't want to ditch her so fast, but I just couldn't handle another moment away from my security blanket as my fear continued to pile up. Linds knew how hard it was for me to say that and could see in my eyes that this was serious.

I called Mom to tell her how my night went. She was already on the road, but now she was on a mission to get to Edmonton. Fear was the magnet that would let nothing keep us apart. "Can Lindsey drive you to Carrie and Jamie's? I'll be there by 2:00 p.m."

I checked the time—three more hours. After the night that had felt like an eternity, three more hours seemed like the longest finish line yet.

"Can you drive me to my mom's friends' place?" I asked Linds as I covered the phone with my hand.

"Yes, absolutely," she replied without a moment's hesitation.

I had never wished time away so quickly in all of my life. All I was concerned about was being reunited with my mom. She was my security blanket and I felt so far outside of my comfort zone without her. Mom was with me through the thick of it all. Every needle prick, every blood test, every palpation, every doctor appointment, every blood transfusion, every swipe of the hair clippers, every exploding vein, and every bag of chemo drugs—she was right by my side. She understood and felt what I was going through with a depth that no one else could have known.

When I got dropped off at our friends', Mom was already there waiting for me and greeted me with a big hug. Carrie and Jamie had been friends with my parents since before I was born. While I hadn't seen them in a long time, I didn't feel the need to wear my armour and pretend everything was okay. Today, more than other days, I did not feel okay, so I didn't pretend to be because it was no use. As we got settled in the spare bedroom, my nerve relaxed a little knowing that Mom was nearby.

My body was aching, and I was so beyond tired. I didn't have any explaining to do as I was sure they could tell by looking at me that I wasn't feeling myself. While less extreme, fear still coursed through my body and consumed my mind, which made me feel distant and closed off. My body was in survival mode considering survival was a top priority at that moment in time. I laid on the couch feeling useless and anti-social while my mom visited with Carrie and Jamie in their dining room.

The look on the ER nurses' faces flashed through my mind. I had travelled this road before and, while I didn't fully grasp the severity of it the last time, knowing what I had been through multiplied my fear tenfold. I knew what came next. Tonight would be the worst night. The fear that was stockpiling in my mind was not helping my body in its attempt to heal.

How long would I let this go on before I finally cracked open? How long would I continue to hold everything inside? When would I finally express my feelings? Would I finally let them out? Or would I let them take me down instead?

My previous belief that strength meant not letting anything affect me was beginning to crack. While I did a decent job of maintaining this fraudulent act on the surface, it didn't change the fact that I was still deeply affected on the inside. A turbulent mess of emotions tossed me around like a kayaker in an ocean storm. Why did I think there was any difference between being externally or internally affected? Who was I trying to hold it together for? And why did I think that mattered so much, anyway? It was a crock of crap. I was growing increasingly sick of my mind bossing me around, telling me how I could and couldn't act.

Then another memory surfaced into my awareness: "Ice queen!" The words echoed in my mind, and I could see myself standing in the hallway of my high school.

"Ice queen!" a friend threw at me jokingly. I furrowed my brows and frowned in response, taken aback.

He laughed at my reaction. I could hear my mental processing out loud. He wasn't the kind of guy to come up with this on his own. He must've heard it from someone else.

"What did you just call me?" I asked, puzzled. "What are you talking about?"

"You're an ice queen!" he repeated.

"What does that even mean?" I responded.

"Nothing ever affects you," he said, smiling.

"Whoa, whoa, whoa. That's not true."

"Yeah, it is. Nothing gets to you. You're like ice. An ice queen!"

Whoa. Is that seriously what he thinks of me? Who else is calling me this? What the hell. Really? I let out a huff of frustration and reflected upon his claim. Huh, shit. I guess that's kind of true.

"Well, at least I'm not a crazy, emotional rollercoaster type of girl, so that's a perk, right?"

"Yep, totally," he confirmed.

Ice queen. The words echoed in my mind.

Am I still being an ice queen? I wondered. That phrase weighed heavy on my heart. Is that what I want to be known as? As tears welled up behind my eyelids, I realized it was high time that definition of self cracked, too.

"You'd better get to bed early tonight, Miss," Mom said with a look of concern, bringing me back from the depths of my wandering mind.

Just get through tonight, then we can go home, I told myself. I nodded in agreement and slowly sat up, allowing my blood flow to normalize to my brain before standing. Waves of dizziness were not uncommon, so I had learned to take it nice and slow before standing up. The last thing I needed was a concussion.

"Wake me up if you need anything in the night," Mom said as she poked her head through the bedroom door.

"Okay," I nodded, knowing it was still very unlikely that I'd actually wake her up. As much as I would have liked to believe I was opening up, I hated to admit vulnerable defeat. I gladly accepted help when it was offered, but still had a hard time reaching out to request it.

I drifted off to sleep in no time but awoke harshly at 2:00 a.m.—the same time as the night before.

Oh. My. God. The aching in my knees had escalated and the pain had travelled to the back of my ankles. My fear levels spiked over what was coming next, and panic moved through my body like a shockwave.

My Cosmic Hammer

Why is this happening? Please, don't let this happen. I can't do this again.

I tried to take deep breaths, to calm my mind, and to allow the pain to decrease and fade, but it was no use. The pain shot my nervous system into emergency mode and my mind raced faster than a car in the Indy 500. The more my fear grew, the more intense the pain got. I needed to get my mind to calm down, but I felt like I had no control over this runaway train. As I writhed in pain, desperation hit me like a tidal wave and allowed the emotional flood gates to open. A steady stream of tears poured down my cheeks, soaking my pillow.

Here I was, back to the torturous pain of feeling like my knees were being ripped apart by a hack saw. *Why? Why is this happening to me?* I begged. I was so devastated. The pain was so unbearable that I could hardly breathe. It ripped me apart on every level of my being.

For two full hours in the middle of the night, I bawled my eyes out, staining the pillow beneath my head as I viciously thrashed my legs. Just when I felt like I had no tears left to cry, the pain would flare back up and a new flood of tears would pour out of my bloodshot eyes.

At 4:00 a.m., I hit my final wall. I had been debating whether to wake Mom or text my BodyTalk practitioner for an emergency session, but I had such a hard time asking for help. Did I believe I didn't deserve help? Was I less worthy if I couldn't handle everything on my own? Did I not want to put anyone out? Underneath it all, it came back to my beliefs about having to be strong and independent. Independence meant I *shouldn't* need help. It meant I *should* be able to handle everything life throws me on my own, and I certainly *shouldn't* get emotional about it. So many lies that I bought as absolute truths.

Eventually, my desperation grew big enough that I threw a Hail Mary and texted Christina at 4:00 a.m. to ask for a BodyTalk session.

Please, please answer. Please answer. I can't do this anymore. I watched the clock roll from 4:00 a.m. to 4:01 a.m., then 4:01 a.m. to 4:02 a.m. which dragged on as the longest minutes of my life.

Please, I begged.

Then, at 4:03 am, she replied: Keep crying. Let those emotions out. Starting your distance session now.

"Oh, thank you, thank you," I replied, while also whispering the words under my breath. I broke into an uncontrollable sob. Help was on the way.

Within the next three minutes, my pain decreased substantially. If my pain had been at a twelve out of ten before, in minutes it dropped down to a three. I could finally breathe. My racing mind calmed down and my legs stopped thrashing.

Why did I wait that long to text Christina? I wondered.

Mom poked her head in. "Are you okay, Miss?" she asked, concerned.

"Well, not really, I've been up since 2:00 a.m. with that same awful knee and ankle pain," I told her with sad, bloodshot eyes and a blotchy, red face.

"Why didn't you wake me up?"

"I don't know. I guess I figured there wasn't anything you could do about it anyway." Logic. Always being so damn logical instead of asking for what my heart needed. My heart needed my momma. Luckily this time, I was comforted by her being in the next room.

"I finally texted Christina five minutes ago and she's doing a session right now. My knees are already starting to feel better."

"Oh, honey." She came to give me a hug. "Do you want me to tap your cortices?"

I nodded, while tears welled up in my eyes once again. I forced a smile as my throat tightened.

"It was probably time you let it all out again, don't you think?"

I nodded again, unable to speak. "Yeah," I squeaked as the tears began to roll down my cheeks yet again. She was right.

Until that point, I hadn't been so sure about the whole distance BodyTalk session thing. But, once again, I got the undeniable confirmation my logical mind so dearly needed. There was no debating that the distance BodyTalk session worked.

As the pain continued to subside, I suddenly became aware of the intensity of fatigue that was taking over my body. Have you ever bawled for two hours straight due to excruciating pain? It's exhausting; never mind barely sleeping the night before and having a body pumped full of chemo chemicals. Before long, I collapsed into sleep out of pure exhaustion.

A wave of relief washed over me the next day as we waved bye and headed home. My muscles relaxed, my clenched jaw released, and I finally put my guard down. It had been exhausting to maintain my composure. But maybe, just maybe, I wasn't supposed to anyway.

On our way home, we stopped in Biggar, Saskatchewan to learn the BodyTalk Access course from Christina. BodyTalk Access is a set of five basic BodyTalk techniques that can be self-administered on a daily basis to significantly improve health. This was the next step on the path to proactive healing.

"When you can't put your feelings into words, when it's not safe to express your truth, your deepest pains, your old hurts... sometimes the body does the job for us. Trying to communicate, trying to find a way to clue us in on what we're feeling and what's going on. Listen to the body. Instead of thinking something is "wrong" with it, ask yourself, "What is it trying to tell me?""
– Nick Ortner

How was it possible for my pain to disappear so quickly when receiving a long-distance healing BodyTalk session in the middle of the night? How could the session provide pain relief within minutes? My practitioner was over 500km away. Trust me, I wondered the same thing. Even though I had already received numerous distance BodyTalk sessions, part of my strong mind still housed pieces of doubt. The pain relief was just another piece of the puzzle that allowed me to trust and believe in the validity and effectiveness of holistic therapies.

Relief came because I finally gave myself permission to surrender to my emotions rather than give in to my typical response of masked strength. In surrendering, I reached out for help. The details that surfaced in my session were rooted in the intensely emotional active memories of my brush with death during my fever emergency on day ten of my previous chemo cycle. As much as I tried to avoid the impending fear of my blood cells bottoming out, my unprocessed fear had grown, which pushed my mind into fight or flight mode and created pain in my body to reflect that fear back to me. I couldn't hold it all in. My body was overflowing with fear and a host of other suppressed emotions. Christina helped me unwind the stifled anxieties of that traumatic memory, along with the emotional buildup that I constantly tried to conceal, the release of which allowed my body's trauma response to subside. As painful as it was, the experience was an opportunity for awareness, learning, and release.

As I mentioned at the start of the book, fear mode is not conducive to healing in any way, shape, or form. Thus, because I had been intensely fighting my thoughts and growing fear, my body was unable to find balance, healing, or sleep. When in fight or flight, the immune system, digestive system, and ability to sleep are the first things to be affected as adrenaline courses through the body, ensuring that every cell is on high alert. No wonder my excruciating pain could not shift, even with the flood of tears that pooled on my pillow.

LOOK GOOD, FEEL BETTER

*"Embrace each challenge in your life as
an opportunity for self-transformation."*
– Bernie Siegel, M.D.

Look Good, Feel Better was a free program offered to cancer patients at the Saskatoon Cancer Centre. The program was meant to help people going through treatment feel better and more confident in themselves through makeup, wig, and hat tutorials.

I first heard about this program when my mom and I were looking for wigs in Saskatoon. To me, anything that would help me *not* look or feel like a cancer patient was music to my ears. However, my nerves sky-rocketed and my armpits grew sweaty as Mom and I found our way to the program room for the event. I hoped I would be the only attendee there so I wouldn't have to reveal my vulnerable baldness to a group of strangers. But, much to my disappointment, the room was filled with over a dozen women, all decades older than me. I awkwardly found my seat, while I tried to blend into my surroundings and sink into my chair.

As the program began, I quietly observed the other attendees and finally realized that, for the first time, I was surrounded by women who were all going through similar experiences, regardless of age. As I witnessed other attendees bravely speak up, ask questions, and share their insecurities, my nerves began to settle.

Much to my surprise, I found the tips and tricks were helpful, and I learned a lot more than I had anticipated, such as: how to landmark and draw on your eyebrows; how to use eyeliner when your eyelashes fall out; how to landmark your (now invisible) hairline for wig placement; hair and hat styles to complement your face shape; how to take care of your skin while on chemo, and much more. While it seemed obvious after hearing it, the instructor explained that having chemo pumped into your body also meant that chemicals would be released through your skin. I learned way more than I had expected and felt relieved in leaving the workshop.

The program was designed to help cancer patients not look so sick so they could feel better and stay positive. If this sounds vain by any stretch of the imagination, then I so kindly invite you to shave off all of your hair, including your eyebrows, pluck out your eyelashes, paint yourself pasty white, and gain fifteen pounds of swelling so you look like a marshmallow. Once complete, go look in the mirror and see how you feel. And then add a cancer diagnosis on top of that. Do you feel me now?

As much as we might not want to admit it, how we perceive ourselves undoubtedly affects how we feel about ourselves. Yes, this is through conditioning from TV, movies, music, commercials, advertising, and beyond, of what is beautiful, fit, healthy, or whatever your definition may be. But, regardless of our conditioning, when we feel better about ourselves, our outlook is more hopeful, our perspective is sunnier, our immune response is stronger, and our resilience is heightened.

This program helped me in ways I could not imagine. It quickly realized the program was not to help cancer patients hide from what they were going through. Sure, in some ways, I used the techniques to hide the heaviness of how I felt. But, at the same time, I saw the instructor with alopecia bravely remove her wig to expose her bare head. I witnessed other cancer patients courageously embracing their new looks, which ever so slightly opened my eyes to the realization that I didn't have to reject my looks, my experience, or myself. By the end of the day, feeling better about myself helped me learn to accept where I was at, what I was going through, and who I was becoming in the process.

BLOODY HELL

"Just keep swimming."
– Dory, Finding Nemo

When I was in high school, I donated blood every time the donor clinic came to town. I always felt proud being able to contribute. However, I never expected to find myself on the receiving end of a blood transfusion, but I guess that's how it goes.

No one usually sees a blood transfusion coming. Blood transfusions are necessary when a person has lost a lot of blood through a traumatic incident, has low blood count due to illness, treatment, or for a host of other medical reasons—chemotherapy being one of them.

In the course of my treatment, I had two blood transfusions. To say this was a scary experience would be a wild understatement. Have you ever watched someone else's blood come down an IV toward your body? It was terrifying.

I vaguely remember my first blood transfusion—it was right before they removed my tumour. Dr. Giede had explained the risks, then recommending that we do it before surgery to prepare my body and help with healing afterwards. The tumour was so large that it was hogging my body's blood supply, which meant that the rest of my body was suffering because of it. While I didn't love the idea of a transfusion, my courage reserves had not yet been depleted, so I had all the gusto to plough through it, no problem. When I had made it to my last round of chemo and my blood count was barely squeaking by. Dr. Giede noted that I needed another blood transfusion to help me make it through the week and stay on schedule to finish out my final round. At that point, I was willing to do whatever it took to stay on schedule and get out of the Cancer Centre so I could head back to school.

Last round, I reminded myself, but I was running out of stamina. And thus, it was the memory of this blood transfusion that jabbed me like a thorn.

Chemo round three, day three.

We were led down the hall and escorted into a quiet room in the Cancer Centre where I would set up camp for the day. This room had a bed, where most of the chemotherapy rooms only had a reclining chair to relax in, which signified I would be there for the long-haul that day. The nurse came in and confirmed my details, blood type, and made sure we knew the risks with blood transfusions. "Sign here," she said after she had listed off the details of informed consent. Once complete, she hooked up the bright red bag of someone else's blood to my IV, then hung it on my IV stand. I was terrified, yet I didn't say a word. Maybe it was my low blood count that contributed to my lack of emotional resilience. Whatever it was, I felt tired, weary, and weak. I could not find an ounce of emotional composure within me. And, honestly, that was okay.

I watched as the blood began to slowly creep its way down the IV tube toward my hand. I knew I desperately needed this lifeline if I was going to stay on schedule with my treatment and get back to college on time. And while I logically understood how vital this blood was to my body, all I could feel was resistance and fear in watching it inch toward my hand.

As it came closer, a panicked feeling took over my body, my chest flooded with emotions, and my heart raced alongside my thoughts. *Whose blood is this?*

When I couldn't take it anymore, I tossed the blanket over my arm and IV, then rolled toward the window where I felt safe to let the tears flow freely without onlookers.

The emotional heaviness had pushed me over my edge. I felt emotionally exhausted and constantly on the verge of tears as my stamina and courage seemed drain from my body. Brought with the emotional overture was an onslaught of traumatic memories from the summer that began to flash through my mind. It had felt like I'd been kicked down and stomped to the ground over and over again in the course of three months. *How much more of this can I take?* I wondered in desperation as tears continued to slide down my cheeks.

After the blood transfusion, I felt gutted and weary, yet was only through the first half of the treatment. Next, we proceeded with the regular schedule of chemo, which crawled by at a snail's pace. By the time it was over, we had been at the Cancer Centre for the majority of the day and I was consumed by exhaustion. As the chemo nurse took my IV out, she smiled and said, "You'll get a new one put in tomorrow."

Oh, thank God..."I get to have a bath tonight," I said as I forced a smile; trying to find the positives.

"You sure do," the nurse replied.

"Two more chemo days," Mom cheered.

Two more days. Two more days. I repeated in my mind. But the thought of two more chemo days felt like an eternity.

A CASE OF THE EXPLODING VEINS

"When you think you've surrendered, surrender some more."
– Gabby Bernstein

I'd made it to day four of my last cycle. Two more days. Two more days. I repeated in my mind. I felt and looked like a puffy, pasty white, marshmallow, which did nothing for my confidence. I was ready for it to be over.

When Mom and I got settled in the room for chemo, a nurse came in with my IV bags and IV supplies and began prepping me for an IV. My veins were much less visible now as compared to my first round, which made it increasingly difficult for the nurses to get my IV in.

Because I only needed three cycles of chemo, I didn't get a port put in my arm to deliver the chemo into my body. Instead, it was delivered intravenously. Since chemo was too hard on the veins to have the IV in the same spot for longer than three days in a row, it meant that I would have an IV in for three days and then have it changed to a new vein on my opposite arm for days four and five of my cycle.

The nurse proceeded to poke the needle through my skin and into a vein in the top of my hand.

"There we go," she said. But as she ran the saline, my hand started to burn.

"Oww! Oww! Oww! That's burning!" I said, as I crinkled my face and clenched my jaw.

"Uh oh. Okay, let's try that again," the nurse said. She tried placing the needle into a slightly different spot but had to poke around a few times to get it. I frowned in discomfort and bit my bottom lip to distract myself from the pain.

"Sorry," she said, "Are you okay?"

"Yeah," I shrugged. "It doesn't feel great, but I'm okay."

"There, let's see how that feels. Here comes the saline."

The burning grew quicker this time. "Oww!" I groaned. *What is happening?!*

"Darn it. The walls of your blood vessels are weakened from the chemo, so your veins keep ballooning, then exploding. Let's try your forearm."

My hand was already getting sore as she moved to attempt two different veins. Four tries and four explosions. No dice. I was getting worried. This feeling reminded me of the fire the Demerol sent coursing up my arm. Shivers ran up my spine at the memory. I took a breath. *Don't think about that now,* I told myself as I changed my focus.

"We will have to slow down the drip pace. I'm going to go see if someone can help me."

She returned with two other nurses. They tried and then tried again. At this point, my poor hands and arms were blowing up like land mines. With every explosion, a bruise formed as a result of the blood pooling underneath my skin. My left hand now felt hard to open and close.

I was running on fumes. Please let this be the last shitty thing I have to go through. I didn't know if I had the stamina to handle another hurdle.

"If we can't get this, we will have to get a hold of your oncologist to see how to proceed. We might have to admit you to inpatient."

Please, no. I closed my eyes and took some deep breaths. The nurses left to figure out what to do. Mom tapped my cortices and we breathed together, as we focused on calming my brain and nervous system to create space for my body's healing protocols to take place.

Imagine being in a triathlon that you haven't trained for. Then, despite the extreme overwhelm and unpreparedness you're feeling while figuring out how to tackle the journey, there is obstacle after obstacle tossed your way—muscle cramps, a downpour of rain, hurdles, a steep incline, sweat burning in your eyes, extreme heat, and a surplus of war wounds that come out of nowhere. This is the only analogy I can use to describe how defeated I felt. I was in the last leg of a brutal triathlon with the finish line up around the bend, yet I was being beat down and running dangerously low on stamina and willpower. I reached down inside myself to gather any remaining shreds of courage I had left within me.

Come on body, we've come this far. We need to finish this. Please, I begged.

Somewhere deep inside of me, I just wanted to be done. I didn't want to have two more days of chemo. Two more days felt like an eternity to my weary soul. I felt swollen, deflated, and emotional. The reflection that stared back at me was not someone I recognized anymore. My face had become puffy and round. My long locks of hair had long since disappeared. The firm, muscular body I had lived in for twenty-one years had become squishy, tired, and weak. My strong legs were now frail, and my thighs had grown puffy. Where six-pack abs once consumed my stomach, now a twelve-inch incision separated it down the middle. Who was this girl looking back at me with the sad eyes? I didn't know her. What I did know was that now was not the time to give up. I had to put down my resistance, set down my fear, and get back up for two more chemo sessions.

Whether I put my guard down and surrendered or mustered all of my courage and determination, I didn't know.

After ten minutes, one of the nurses came back. "Let's try this one more time," she said, confidently. "We've got to get this in."

"Eighth try's a charm?" I offered, trying to make light of the situation to release the stress we were all feeling.

"Hold your arms straight with your hands toward the floor. Let's find the best vein you have."

I leaned forward in the chair and followed her directions. "There it is. This one's the one," she said. I smiled and took a deep breath.

This is the one, I confirmed in my mind. This is the one.

"Here we go," she said. "Got it. Now, nice and easy."

Deep breaths, eyes closed, here we go, body. Here we go. We've got this.

She turned on the saline. When I wanted to hold my breath to wait for the explosion, I took a breath instead to interrupt my expectation. I just kept focusing on my breath. All the way in and all the way out. In and out.

After a few moments, I opened my eyes. The nurse looked at me with her eyebrows raised. "Good?" she asked, with both of her thumbs up.

I paused before responding. "Yeah, it is," I smiled. "No burning."

"YES!" she cheered, "Please don't move. We don't want that coming out." She said as she gently taped the tubes to my arm more carefully than any nurse had ever done before.

"Thank you," I said relieved. I felt as though I had just collapsed over the finish line. Relief washed over me. By the time she left, I was exhausted and emotionally drained. I looked down at my poor arms—covered in bruises.

"Look," I said to Mom, motioning toward my arms.

"Ouch," she said empathetically. "Maybe you should have a sleep. It'll help this go by quicker."

I nodded and closed my eyes, even as they began welling up with tears. I felt like I had made it to the home stretch. I would go as slowly as I needed to, but I would not stop.

In my mind, thoughts wandered and unwound as I tried to calm myself enough to drift off to sleep. I was so tired, but my mind was on the move. Just rest, I told myself. While I felt wiped out by the experience, I was also full of gratitude and relief. Exhaustion seemed to loosen the emotional gates I usually kept locked up tight. Tears softly welled then gently drifted down my cheeks.

Why did it work the eighth time?

Was it because the nurse didn't have two other nurses hovering over top of her watching her every move? Was it because there was an ultimatum of being admitted to inpatient? Was it because I finally let my guard down and surrendered? Or because I mustered enough courage to get back up? Had the cortices technique helped to calm my nervous system? Was it because we interrupted fear? Or, was it all of the above?

I believe that this lesson came to show me how fear can affect our bodies. Sure, I'd been through the ringer—there was no doubt about that. But in the midst of such trying times, I had to surrender my fear and control. Since both were triggering survival mode, it meant that neither were helping me heal. Surrender. Let go. Trust. Breathe. Calm the ego. Get out of your own way. Then sit back and witness everything fall into place just as it was always meant to.

HOMESTRETCH HALLELUJAH

My final day of chemo came and went without a hitch. Inside, I felt a mixture of nervousness, relief, and exhaustion. Peace out, Cancer Centre! I was so happy I could have cried. The last obstacle in my way was day ten. As much as I wanted to believe that I'd already passed my last hurdle, the thought of day ten scared me more than I wanted to admit.

I had two weeks of recovery before my final appointment where I hoped to get Dr. Giede's stamp of approval to head back to college. My excitement was palpable and freedom coursed through my veins. My textbooks had been delivered, and I was eager to get started. Never had I been so nerd-level excited to dive into my schoolwork—and I usually was pretty excited, so that was saying something. I did everything in my power to support myself through this process. Having school to look forward to sparked an accelerated drive to heal.

With freedom in sight, coupled with the blood transfusion and numerous GCSF injections, my blood count managed to hold its own against the chemo this time. Day ten brought some mild aching, but nothing like the excruciating pain of the two previous rounds.

Mom, Dad, and I excitedly walked into the Cancer Centre for my final checkup with Dr. Giede on September 19th—the Wednesday of my final week of recovery. After reviewing my blood work and discussing next steps, I exchanged a glance of excitement with my parents.

I looked at Dr. Giede with anticipation and asked, "So, am I good to go back to school then?"

He paused, then looked at Kathy, my parents, and then finally back at me. I raised my eyebrows awaiting his verdict. Finally, his words hit my eardrums.

"I don't see why you can't. As long as you're willing to continue your checkups in Niagara, then I don't have a problem with that."

"YES!" I squealed. "Oh, absolutely, I will," I reassured him. "Good thing you said yes because we have flights booked for tomorrow morning," I told him with a gritted-tooth smile, as if I was waiting to get in trouble.

"Oh, okay then. You guys don't waste any time, do you?" he said, with a look of surprise plastered all over his face. By now, he knew I wouldn't take no for an answer. Going back to school was my drive—to be reunited with my team, my friends, my roommates. Getting back into the routine of being a "normal" college student was what I had been aiming for all summer.

"You'll have to come back and see me when you are home for Christmas."

"Of course, I will," I said as I did a seated happy dance on the exam table.

Mom reassured him that she had already booked my scheduled appointments in Niagara, that she was travelling with me, and that my dad would be driving my car down. We were all in—just like we had always been. Whatever it took. I was ready for my next stage of healing: reintegration into real life.

"Alright then. Well, our work here is done." Dr. Giede gave me a high five; then, my parents and I profusely thanked him and Kathy for their guidance on this heart-wrenching journey. They were our co-pilots through scary, uncharted territory and we'd finally made it through the storm.

"We can't thank you both enough. We are so grateful, and we are so proud of her," Mom choked out, as Kathy gave her a hug.

Dad blinked back tears as he shook Dr. Giede's hand.

They all seemed grateful and proud of our triumphant completion. As we hugged and congratulated each other in that office in the Cancer Centre, I felt like I could finally exhale a sigh of relief. The final nod of completion gave me permission to truly celebrate. I'd officially crossed the finish line that I had been begging for all summer. It seemed surreal to have finally made it, but I couldn't have been more relieved and more excited to turn the page.

It was a bittersweet departure. These two had been brought into my life under the harshest of circumstances, and now it was time for us to part ways, forever changed, to embark on the next leg of our journeys.

FIRST TASTE OF FREEDOM

The next morning, I rose bright and early, eager to board the plane and leave the whole experience in the rear view. We checked in at the airport, dropped our luggage, and hugged Dad; then waved as we disappeared through the security checkpoint.

The day was finally here—the day that I'd been aiming for throughout all of the trials and tribulations of the longest summer of my life. Yet, it all seemed to fade away as we made our way toward our gate.

The past three months had been full of heartache, fear, struggles, and more love than my heart could hold, but I was so ready to get the hell away from all of it. It was time for this chapter to come to an end. While I still had a long way to go, my healing journey officially began the moment the gate agent scanned my plane ticket and I started down the long jetway to board the plane.

My eyes filled with tears and relief flooded through my body as I reflected on the size of this momentous occasion. If there was ever any doubt in my mind that I couldn't handle what life threw my way, today was the day that it vanished forever. I had reached the summit of the most difficult experience I would ever endure. I could finally breathe.

I had packed up my hurting heart, my broken body, my headstrong mind, and my relentless determination, ready to turn the page and finish what I'd started: my degree. Little did I know, I was returning to school with a brand-new outlook on life and a transformed perspective on health.

PART THREE:

Connecting the Dots

"She was never weak, but had to be shown her strength in a way she would never doubt. The Universe took a cosmic hammer, mercilessly, to all that she knew. As pieces of her fell like confetti, they revealed the secrets they hide. Presenting themselves as gifts, she realized the cosmic hammer was a butterfly flapping its wings."

- t.m.t

WESTERN MEDICINE SAVED MY LIFE

*"You have the power to heal yourself, and you need to know that.
We think so often that we are helpless, but we're not. We always have
the power of our minds. Claim and consciously use your power."*
– Louise Hay

Western medicine saved my life. It was true. By the time I arrived home for the summer, my tumour was too advanced to be able to deal with it in any other way. Other organs were being affected by the sheer size of the tumour, which began to wreak havoc throughout my body. While the doctors didn't think my symptoms were related to anything more than constipation, I knew that something was off within my body. Like I mentioned, doctors are human, just like everyone else. If you ever feel like your doctor isn't "hearing" you, then please get another opinion. Then, check out some holistic therapies while you're at it. While chemo is by far the toughest experience I have ever endured, and at times I wonder if I physically needed it, I found an incredible amount of growth in the trials and tribulations that chemo brought forth.

Western medicine saved my life when my kidneys grew toxic, when I had a tumour growing inside of me that was the size of a football, and when my blood counts reached an all-time low. In these moments, I absolutely needed the help of trained medical professionals. There is always a time and a place for medical care. It can be the difference between life and death. It can be what saves a life.

While, western medicine saved my life, physically, it was not what helped me heal.

BodyTalk helped me heal on every level of my being—physically, mentally, emotionally, and spiritually—which was far more beneficial than I could have ever expected. My BodyTalk sessions and practitioner helped me get connected with myself as I began to wake up to the messages from my body. BodyTalk helped my bodymind find balance even in the darkest of days. It helped me with pain management, emotional release, making sense of my symptoms, my mental health, and showed me that hiding behind a mask of strength was not necessarily a good thing.

In creating new awareness, BodyTalk opened my mind to a new perspective on health, which helped me understand the importance of listening to my body, honouring its messages and wisdom, and the realization that my mind, body, and emotions are all interconnected. The modality was a godsend that opened my mind, my heart, and my eyes to connect with myself more deeply than I ever had before. It was the bridge that introduced me to my whole self, and am I forever grateful to have stumbled upon this awareness at such a pivotal time in my life.

BodyTalk opened my mind to the fact that, as humans, we are so much more than just physical bodies. The body works together as one big, magical machine to maintain balance and harmony. Meaning that one's spiritual, mental, and emotional states cannot be separated from the connection with the physical body. BodyTalk honours the body's innate intelligence, realizing that the body always has and always will know how to heal itself in the appropriate healing sequence, if only we would get our mind and emotions out of the way.

Your body was built to heal. And this magnificent machine that we are blessed to reside in is always communicating and reflecting that which we are feeling, thinking, and holding inside. It sends us quiet messages in the form of whispers, feelings, hunches, ideas, and if we aren't paying attention, those nudges can grow into symptoms, injuries, ailments, and disease.

If you consider these insights with an open mind, you may realize that your recent stomach ache started when you began worrying about an upcoming presentation, that your knees begin to hurt when you are overcome with fear or are stubbornly standing your ground, that your shoulders feel heavy and sore when you feel mentally and emotionally burdened with responsibilities, or that your headache comes on when you're internally overthinking a comment from your boss. Our bodies send us messages *all of the time,* if only we could pay attention, honour, and trust the body's wisdom and attempts to clue us in on how we're feeling.

"Once in a while It really hits people that they don't have to experience the world in the way they have been told to."
— Alan Keightly

THE MEANING OF CANCER

"You must master a new way to think
before you can master a new way to be."
– Marianne Williamson

Body consciousness relates to the fact that each part of the body has a job that it does, physically, emotionally, and/or metaphorically. The shoulders carry our responsibilities. When we feel burdened by our responsibilities, this can show up as muscular tension, physical injuries or affect our posture. The knees are about will power. When we lock our knees, we are either being stubborn or attempting to stand in our power. When we bend our knees to pray, we give up our power and surrender. More than just body parts, emotions, symptoms and illness also have a metaphorical purpose.

According to Louise Hay's book, *You Can Heal Your Body*, "Cancer represents deep hurt, longstanding resentment, and carrying hatred that literally eats away at the body."

Do you remember the ice queen story? Talk about stuffing emotions down for the better part of my life.

When we hold our emotions in, our body has to store them somewhere. As the first law of thermodynamics states, "Energy cannot be created nor destroyed, only transferred or changed from one form to another." So, when it comes to emotional energy, if it is not expressed or released in one way or another, then the body files it away for safe keeping. Unfortunately, this is not helpful or healthy for the body or the mind because this emotional energy blocks the body's ability to physically function at an optimal level. As this energy continues to be held internally, it builds up, creating blockages that will eventually turn into pain, symptoms, illness, and disease.

All emotions have a purpose—a reason that they show up—and they are meant to move through the bodymind to be released. Certain emotions are apt to be stored in certain areas of the body, which I've always found fascinating. Anger tends to show up in the liver, gall bladder, jaw and fists. Fear tends to be stored in the bladder, kidneys, psoas, and knees. Worry shows up in the stomach and the spleen. Grief usually surfaces in the lungs, chest, and large intestine.

Each emotion has a reason for when and where it surfaces. For example, anger is supposed to cause movement. When it is held in, the pressure builds until an explosion occurs—either physically (say, in the form of a vertebral disc rupture), emotionally (in the form of an emotional outburst), or mentally (perhaps in the form of a nervous breakdown). When held inside, these emotions begin to eat away at us, weakening our immune systems, wearing on our mental state, and stockpiling in our organs and tissues. When the body is carrying the stuck emotional energy that was only ever meant to move through us, it overloads the organs, endocrines, systems, and tissues, thus impeding their ability to function optimally. Emotions were never meant to be carried.

In my case, this made a whole lot of sense. While I didn't often overreact on the surface, I rode an emotional rollercoaster internally where I would constantly judge myself and beat myself up for having emotions. I did what it took to remain stoic on the surface. This was not a healthy way to live. Physical activity was my stress reliever, which was better than not doing anything, but it was a huge avoidance tactic to escape from how I really felt on the inside. And as Brene Brown says, "We cannot selectively numb emotions. When we numb the painful emotions, we also numb the positive emotions."

Ovaries represent the point of creation, creativity, and femininity. In terms of creativity, I've held a longstanding belief that I am not creative. I struggled in art class, likely due to my overpowering logical mind, and I thought creativity was pointless. I could not see the magic of creativity and artistic expression, so I completely disregarded that aspect of myself. Plus, to be creative requires an open mind, which I didn't truly have at the time. That being said, I believe there is much more to creativity than just art. Creativity is a magic in itself. It is believing in the unseen, the not-yet-imagined, and the power of possibility, ideas, and imagination. Creativity is self-expression. It is sharing one's heart and the workings of one's mind. To be creative is to be vulnerable, which helps me understand why I closed myself off from connecting with creativity. By not believing I was creative, I was abandoning a much bigger part of my self than I could have ever imagined.

Regarding the point of creation and femininity, there was a laundry list of limiting beliefs beneath my rejection of emotional expression, vulnerability, femininity, dependence, and being nurtured. My experiences had led me to believe that expressing emotions equated to dramatic overreactions, weakness, and volatility which I mentally tied to the feminine and were not traits I aspired to have. This led to a major rejection of all aspects of femininity within myself and the world around me. Instead, I appreciated the masculine qualities of being steady, logical, intelligent, and athletic because they were safer. Diving deeper, my experience of generational mother/daughter issues likely played a role in my perspective of femininity, which is a divine opportunity for healing that I will continue to investigate and unravel.

Now, I could blame myself for holding my emotions in. I could berate myself for deserving cancer. And for a while, I did. But now I can truly see that I have always been doing the best I can from my level of understanding. Like most youth, I firmly adopted learned facts and experiences as absolute truths without questioning them, which created an incredibly tight, rigid mental box and viewpoint of reality. No wonder I needed to have it smashed to bits. Cancer happened *for* me to open me up, help me work through my attachments, and collapse the harsh ideals and perspectives I had of myself that were just not working. I didn't know any better until I did. And now, with a deeper understanding of self, I can choose a kinder, more compassionate, and open-minded approach towards myself and the world around me.

While my understanding has come a long way, I am still unpacking old emotional baggage, unraveling outdated beliefs, learning to allow my emotions to flow freely, and unlearning the self-talk that surfaces in my mind. Unraveling this experience will never be finished because my understanding of self is not absolute, nor will it ever be. It is like the perpetual peeling of the paper-thin layers off an onion. I will continue to find new awareness and heal this experience for the rest of my life.

THE OTHER SIDE

"Life's challenges aren't supposed to paralyze you,
they're supposed to help you discover who you are."
– Bernice Johnson Reagon

When I came out on the other side of my experience with cancer, I let out an exhale of utter relief. I had made it out of the woods. Being in survival mode for so long, I was purely focused on making it through chemo so I could return to college for my final year. I didn't take the time to emotionally process everything that I went through, except during my BodyTalk sessions. Thank goodness there were a lot of them.

When I returned to college, I felt like a foreigner in the life I used to live. *Who am I now?* I knew I couldn't just go back to who I was before. But who was I now? Did I even know who I was before? I couldn't pretend that my summer hadn't smashed everything I thought I knew about myself into smithereens.

Coming out alive on the other side of a deadly illness is like staring at the remains of your home after a debilitating storm has torn it to shreds. When the dust settles, you are standing on the other side of the experience emotionally steamrolled and mentally in shambles. It is surreal—so much so that you wonder if the entire experience even happened or if it is just an awful dream.

Who are you after you make it through to the other side of trauma? Whether that be physical, mental, emotional, sexual, or spiritual trauma—there is major processing that needs to be done. This is not to say that all trauma is equal—or maybe it is, of that, I don't know. I can only speak from my experience. Everyone experiences trauma in their lifetimes—but it's what you do afterwards that counts.

I know now that cancer was a gift for me, and it also could be for others who are willing to open their minds too. What if all extreme happenings are wake up calls sent to get your attention? What if you actually needed a wild awakening to give yourself permission to find what lights your fire, to let go of all that squishes your soul, and to heal the wounded parts of you?

To say the summer of 2007 was transformative for me would be a wild understatement. I was stretched, pushed, and tossed into uncharted and uncomfortable territory time after time. My once beautiful stomach now had a twelve-inch scar that ran around my belly button and divided my abdomen right down the middle to my pubic bone. My long, thick, blonde hair that had once flowed past my shoulders had vanished in the blink of an eye.

In hindsight, it is clear now that I lost my identity. I lost every piece of myself that I was so strongly attached to—my physical body, my medical understanding, my hair, my athleticism, my physical strength, my definition of health, and my definition of self. Instead, I questioned everything I thought I knew which was exactly what this disease was always meant to spark within me. I found myself at a crossroads, leaving behind who I was and moving into who I was meant to become.

As Paulo Coelho said, "Maybe the journey isn't so much about becoming anything. Maybe it's about unbecoming everything that isn't really you, so you can be who you were meant to be in the first place."

MY WAKE-UP CALL

"Feeling the need to be busy all the time is a trauma response
and fear-based distraction from what you'd be forced
to acknowledge and feel if you slowed down."
— *Maxine Carter*

Did I actually need chemo? Of that I'm not sure. Did I truly need to have those chemicals pumped into my body as "insurance" to not get cancer again? Maybe not. But, one thing I know for certain was that I needed the wake-up call of chemotherapy.

If I'd only needed surgery, I would have continued on my merry way with only a giant scar running down my abdomen. That wasn't the transformation the Universe had in store for me. The wake-up call that I had ordered up was much more potent than that, and I wasn't about to get off so easily. I needed the full-meal-deal in order to really stop, reflect, reassess my life, and take a good hard look in the mirror.

Surgery wouldn't have stopped me. Surgery alone wouldn't have forced me to slow down to a crawl. This "slow down" was a big deal for a girl who constantly had a full plate, a busy schedule, and had learned early on how to try to juggle everything. Chemo was the miracle that made my "normal" way of life all come crashing down. The unconscious way that I had been functioning was not a sustainable way to live my life. Yes, I had always been a high achiever, striving for more, but this experience taught me how to slow down, pause, rest, and reset, which was something that I had almost entirely forgotten how to do.

This slowing down created an incredible space to get to know myself, learn to listen to my body, honour my soul, and realize that I didn't have to always strive to be an invincible superhero.

Being forced to slow down helped me lean into the uncomfortable reality of not only needing help, but asking for it, accepting support, and not being physically able to press on.

I needed that wakeup call.

Cancer softened me. Maybe not immediately, but it broke open my hardened protective shell, allowing me to move inward to explore and heal through layers upon layers of my metaphorical personal onion.

I have come a long way in the last thirteen years, yet I know this is only the beginning because we are never done unlearning for as long as we live. But, I am ever so grateful for the catalyst that began the unfolding process—unbecoming all that I am not, so I could discover and uncover the real me under the masks, beliefs, labels, roles, and all the other bullshit I came to believe about myself over the years. It woke me up to my innate wisdom and my inborn gifts and talents, while redirecting my career path and my entire life, and infusing me with an aligned purpose that resonates deep within my soul.

If I'd faced something less extreme than cancer, I wouldn't have woken up to find a new way to live my life. I wouldn't have gotten the message if I wasn't dealt something life-shattering. This experience changed everything for me, just like it was supposed to. It was the cosmic hammer that smashed me on the head and woke me up to a new way of being, thinking, and experiencing life. It redirected my entire life and opened my eyes to the magnificent wisdom I have always had within myself and had been ignoring for most of my life. It showed me there was so much more to the human experience than the physical body.

This journey has been nothing short of mind-blowing and transformational, at a level so deep that words will never do it justice—connecting the cosmic dots and making my whole world make sense. Thank you to the angel in a nursing uniform who listened to her intuition and told my family about BodyTalk on that fateful day, in a hospital room in Rosetown, Saskatchewan.

Life-altering events are *supposed* to alter your life. They are *supposed* to wake you up. They are *supposed* to make you question everything you think

Kristin Pierce

you know. But, luckily, you do not need cancer or any other cosmic hammer to pause, reflect, and re-evaluate your life. You are fully capable of doing so whenever you choose. So, why wait for a cosmic hammer to force you to get honest with yourself? I highly recommend incorporating a regular dose of self-reflection and re-evaluation into your self-care routine.

MOMENTS

"You can rise up from anything. You can completely recreate yourself. Nothing is permanent. You're not stuck. You have choices. You can think new thoughts. You can learn something new. You can create new habits. All that matters is that you decide today and never look back."
– Idil Ahmed

There are moments in life that make you question everything. Moments that break you, moments that make you, moments that change you in an instant, and moments that will be forever etched into your memory. There are times in your life when it feels as though everything is falling apart. Where life shatters right before your eyes and you feel as if you are witnessing the experience from above while your beating heart is ripped from your chest and you are blindsided by a freight train all at once.

You are left holding in your hands the shattered pieces of your life; so sharp you can feel the warm, metaphorical blood seeping from your fresh wounds. It takes every ounce of strength to pick yourself back up—every ounce of courage to put one foot in front of the other when you'd rather lie collapsed in a heap on the floor.

When standing with the broken, shattered pieces of your life in your hands, there is the most remarkable opportunity—a crossroads, if you will—to wake up and find a new way. It is an opportunity to rebuild yourself from scratch, a silver lining to uncover. In every struggle, there is a beautiful gift waiting for you when you are ready, willing, and open to receiving it. A message in the mess, a gift in the wound. As difficult as it may be to hear this, all of life is happening for you, not to you. Within the raw reality of these moments lies a powerful opportunity to ask yourself some big questions. After all, is that not the underlying purpose of a cosmic hammer?

Why am I here?

Is this what life's all about?

Am I happy with how my life is unfolding?

If not, what am I going to do about it?

If I had to pick one key takeaway from that summer of cancer, it would be this: your soul is your inner compass. When it feels unsettled, squished, or off-kilter, it's because you are veering off track. Get reconnected. Go spend some time alone with yourself. Listen to your soul. Find out who you are, what you stand for, and why you're here. Because it matters. And you matter.

"You should give a fuck. You really should. But only about things that set your soul on fire. Save your fucks for magical shit."
– Fuckology

ACKNOWLEDGEMENTS

"Growth is often uncomfortable, messy,
and full of emotions you weren't expecting."
– Molly Ho

To my family, friends, cousins, aunts, uncles, grandparents, and everyone who visited me in the hospital, at home, or who sent cards, flowers, gifts, emails, well wishes and more, thank you. All of your support during the most difficult experience of my life helped me to believe in myself when I needed it most.

Mom and Dad: Thank you for believing in me without a shadow of a doubt, for helping me take my health into my own hands, and for doing everything in your power to help and support me that summer, before, and beyond.

Kenton and Kiel and Chantel: You all brought me comfort in your presence. Thank you for simply being around, being goofballs, and for always giving me a reason to laugh.

Mark: Thank you for opening my heart. I am grateful for our time together, and I am so thankful for your friendship, your support, and the incredible lessons.

Linds: Thank you for helping me laugh until my cheeks hurt, sing my heart out, and open up about everything under the sun. Your support still brings me to tears.

Landon: I appreciate your courage and kindness in inviting me to attend the wedding with you. It may have seemed like a small gesture for you, but it was incredibly impactful for me. That adventure and your friendship mean so much to me.

Schar and Brittany: Thank you for helping me find my inner spitfire and for always believing in me.

Kev: Thanks for showing up and being there for me. Your presence meant a lot, even if we weren't able to talk about the hard stuff. I will always cherish our friendship.

Meds: Thank you for the visits that summer and your unconditional friendship, acceptance, and support. It meant, and still means, a lot.

Christine: Thanks for being such a good friend. You helped in any way you could and I appreciated your presence and support.

To my Mercyhurst besties, roommates, teammates, coaches, friends, and teachers, your encouragement and support helped me keep my chin up and inspired me to keep my eye on my goal of returning to Erie.

Christina: Thank you for sharing your gifts, wisdom, understanding, compassion, and support with me. Thank you for opening my mind to a new perspective of health, the body, and the mind and for teaching me that my ideas of "strength" were all wrong. I am so eternally grateful our paths crossed.

Kathy: You were a safe haven in the midst of a terrible storm. Thank you for carefully answering our millions of questions, for being our steady ground as we attempted to find our footing, and for supporting all of our alternative healthcare choices. Your unconditional support softened the blow of all the terrifying aspects of chemo.

Dr. Giede: It's hard to put into words how to thank you. I know it wasn't your typical nature to be emotionally vested in your patients, so thank you for caring for me as if I was your own. You helped us navigate through the most difficult experience with confidence and clarity. Thank you for getting excited with us when I was ready to be freed from the Cancer Centre.

Evelyn: Thank you for trusting your gut enough to tell us about BodyTalk when we so desperately needed some hope. Although our interaction was brief, it is forever etched into my mind. Thank you for teaching us that we didn't have to leave my fate to the statistics before we even found out what those statistics were.

Dr. Dion: You are such a kind, sweet soul. Thank you for your kindness, empathy, and tears. You showed me that it was okay for doctors to be emotional, to be human. I am grateful to have had you as my family doctor.

Lacy: Thank you for unmatched guidance in helping me get this book out to the world. Your expertise, dedication, support, and enthusiasm have helped me in more ways than I can accurately articulate. Thank you for letting me bounce ideas off you and for helping me organize my thoughts. I truly respect your opinion and appreciate you.

Kyla: Thank you for your support in helping me unravel my thoughts, emotions, and beliefs as I worked through writing this book. I treasure our friendship.

Aspen and Kendrix: Thank you for choosing me as your mom, you beautiful souls. It is a gift to get to learn from and with you both everyday. Thank you for your love, hugs, support, and snuggles, and for asking the best questions to help guide me through sharing this story Always remember your bodies are healing machines, your minds are magical, and feelings are meant to be felt. Love you both to the moon and back.

Matt: Your unwavering support and encouragement never ceases to amaze me. Thank you for being my sounding board, for picking up the slack around the house while I spent endless hours at my computer, for your confidence and belief in me, and for not letting me give up on this book, but also knowing when I needed the freedom to find my way back to it. Thank you for being you. Thank you for growing with me. I love you.

Kristin and Diesel, 2007.

ABOUT THE AUTHOR:

Kristin Pierce is a mindset and self-awareness educator , a self-empowerment speaker, and the founder of Inner Compass Academy where she empowers others to deconstruct their self-limiting beliefs that keep them small and stuck in order to rise to their potential, come alive, and impact the world. She loves asking questions, stretching her comfort zone, and encouraging her students and clients to shift their perspectives, open their minds, and expand their awareness of mind, body, and self. She is a MindScape Instructor, an Advanced Certified BodyTalk Practitioner, a BodyTalk Access Instructor, a Registered Massage Therapist, and a trained acupuncturist. She holds a Bachelor of Science in Sports Medicine from Mercyhurst College in Erie, Pennsylvania.

Kristin is an award-winning and Amazon best-selling children's author and the founder of Inner Compass Books where it is her mission to create mindfully crafted children's books that encourage kids to question their limits, trust their intuition, pursue their passions, and dream bigger than belief. Her titles include *Your Inner Compass That Could, Mayva O'Meere, Creationeer, Magnus O'Meere, Mind Pioneer,* and *The Sweet Dreams Express: A Meditative Bedtime Journey.* Her upcoming titles include *Hazel Mist, Hypnotist* and *Anxious Annie Unwinds Her Mind.* Visit www.InnerCompassBooks.com to learn more or find her books on Amazon.

Kristin lives in Saskatchewan, Canada with her husband, Matt, two children, Aspen and Kendrix, and their dog.

You can find Kristin on Facebook and Instagram @InnerCompassAcademy, on her blog, and on her website at www.InnerCompassAcademy.com

Made in the USA
Monee, IL
30 October 2020

45769551R00138